Weak and Loved

Scripture quotations are from
The Holy Bible, English Standard Version® (ESV®),
copyright © 2001 by Crossway, a publishing ministry of Good News
Publishers.
All rights reserved.

Cover photo by Michele Lee Rockhill.
http://jmrockhill.blogspot.com

ISBN: 1-4664-8431-4
ISBN-13: 9781466484313

Weak and Loved

A Mother-Daughter Love Story

Emily Cook

For more by Emily Cook including the latest on Aggie
please visit http://www.weakandloved.com

Contents

Acknowledgments

This book would not have been possible without the editorial work of Kathy Klumpp. I owe you a great debt for your diligent and patient correction of this manuscript. I thank God for providing you as an editor, friend, and soulmate in motherhood. Pastor Brandt, Pastor Rich Shields, Beth Beck, Karen Higgins, Tara Haley, Amy Orban, Rebekah Curits, and Amy Sievert: I am deeply grateful for your feedback and encouragement. God knows I need a rich supply.

Many thanks to Dr. Elaine Wyllie, Dr. William Bingaman, and the countless medical professionals at Cleveland Clinic. Thank you for using your talents to serve others. You were God's hands of healing for Aggie. Without you this would have been a much different story.

To the many people who upheld our family in prayer, supported us with words and soup, and made certain we were never alone in our sadness: how could I ever thank you enough? Our church family at White Creek served us as the body of Christ and showered us with grace and love in our season of weakness. Your kindnesses were relentless reminders of God's care for us even in suffering.

I also thank God for our dear family members who loved and suffered along with us. Aggie, even when she was sick, soaked up constant love from her Grammy Pammy, Larry-Bump, Nana, and Bump, and so many others. Thank you for supporting her, and her parents, and showing us how to love whatever Aggie we were given each day.

Mom and Dad, where would I be without your constant love? You can never stop me loving you either.

I am deeply grateful for the friendship and help of Mary Anne Schneider. She loves all Cooks, healthy or sick; noisy or destructive; big or little. Aunt Mary Anne, we are so glad you are part of our family.

Aggie Sue: I am so glad for every day God has given us with you. Through you, God is still teaching me to be weak and loved. You will always be my Agnes, pointing upward, just like your namesake.

Joshua: I am glad you finally forced yourself to read this book all the way to the end before it was published! I know my words bring up emotions you would rather forget. Your love upheld me through this trial and many others. You are truly a picture of God's grace to me. I hope to harass you with my emotional words for many years to come.

And finally, thanks be to God, who loves the weak.

Dedicated to Vivian Anastasia Gregory

Luther's prayer based on
"Cast all your care upon God, for He cares for you."
1 Peter 5:7

Heavenly Father, You are indeed my Lord and God,
who has created me when I was but nothing.
In addition, You have saved me through Your Son.
Now You have appointed me to this official responsibility
and set this work before me.
It does not proceed according to my will,
and it is so great that it would otherwise weigh heavily on me and
cause me great fear,
that I of my own ability could find neither counsel nor help.
Therefore, let everything be commended unto You,
give me counsel and help, and remain faithful in everything,
as You have promised.
Amen.[1]

Chapter 1
Autumn

"September 25, 2008
"To Agnes on her fourth birthday,

"My hummingbird, my tornado, my whirlwind! Sometimes you have so much energy in your little body that it seems to shoot out of your fingertips and make your hair stand on end!

"What you were like at age four: Yesterday, you bounced out of bed at 6 a.m. ready to go and full of spunk. You stayed in your pajamas and curled up with your teddy bear blanket on the couch, drinking chocolate milk and watching Curious George, Sid the Science Kid, and Super Why. (You can tell I was very tired that morning because you got to watch all three of your favorite shows!) During breakfast you wiggled, ate, wiggled, argued with Seth, wiggled some more, fell out of your chair, then finally finished eating. You got yourself dressed, made your bed, and brushed your teeth in about 30 seconds flat. You are always so eager to start the day and ready for absolutely anything! Yesterday, I didn't quite get around to brushing your hair, so you ran around all day with the sides sticking out and up and what looked like a bird's nest on the back of your head. Nonetheless, you spent most of the day feeling pretty in your dress up costumes. I love the way you dress up like a princess and even a "wedding girl" while all the time insisting that you are NEVER going to get married and NEVER going to have babies.

"Yesterday, like every day, you made adventures for yourself. You swung on a door and broke it off its hinges. You broke a mini-blind; or, as you explained when you humbly handed me the pieces, "Mommy, this was just sitting on the floor and it broke!" Then, you saw Marcus in the bathtub enjoying the warm water as it filled.

When I turned my back for one second, you quietly turned the water to COLD and casually walked out of the room. It took about five minutes and a good deal of complaining from Marcus for me to figure out what was wrong. As I write this, you are feeding your baby doll "mommy milk" in the sandbox.

"You and your big sister, Lorraine, are very close friends. Your favorite things to do with Lorraine are to play dress up, do crafts, paint, stay up late and giggle with her, or drive her nuts while she is trying to sleep. Lorraine does not always understand your love for noise and adventure! Seth is more like you in that way. Some days you create joyful chaos with your younger brother; other days, you turn your chaotic energy against each other and do nothing but fight. You love to tease everyone at all times, just like your daddy. Your favorite insults at the moment include, "Seth is a poopy diaper!" and, "Rainy is a piggy princess!" You and Daddy both find great joy in harassing everyone else in the family!

"You are still in love with your baby brother Marcus. You get such a kick out of his little developments, especially when they are clumsy or messy or loud. I remember your belly laugh when Marcus was trying to figure out how to use a sippy cup for the first time. You melted my heart when you said, "Marcus is slobbering on my teddy bear blanket, and it's ok with me if he does that."

"You add chaos, adventure, and lots of laughter to our family. You have a huge heart, even for your sister and brothers, and you relish any time you can share anything, from a piece of candy to a party with others. I imagine you look at almost every situation and wonder, "How can I make this more fun?" I cannot begin to imagine what God has in store for you as an adult. Perhaps you are one of those kids who really will grow up to be an astronaut or an airplane pilot! As I watch you live each day you remind me to rejoice in the present, to take every day as a gift of God, like a full glass of your favorite drink, chocolate milk. You drink every last drop, use the energy to have adventures all day, and finally collapse into bed exhausted.

"Happy fourth birthday Aggie Sue! We surely do love you!"

I am glad I took the time to write that letter when I did. I treasure it now, as it holds a glimpse of the little girl we loved before everything changed. I wish I could recall the last normal day that I had with the children. What did we do? Did we spend the day reading books, going to the park, doing crafts, and taking long naps? Did I take time to listen to their laughter? Did I soak up their hugs and kisses or did I just hurry them off to bed? Did I even notice that sparkle in Aggie's eye? Did I listen to her jokes or was I too busy? Was there a hint that our lives were about to change forever, some sort of a sign or clue that I missed? Was there something that should have told me to take more pictures, to listen more, to soak up the everyday hugs just a little longer?

The leaves began to change colors and fall from the trees. Everyone marveled at the quick passing of summer, just as they do every year, and I marveled along with them. Yes, of course, hints of change were everywhere, but like everyone else, I paid no attention. I was surrounded by warm, uneventful days, but I did not store away any bright pieces of life or health for the future. Winter was on its way, but I had no idea how cold it was about to become, or how quickly.

Chapter 2
Silence Invades

October, 2008

We were at the park when I saw Aggie's first "episode."

The "school park," as the children called it, was one of their favorite things about our new home in southern Indiana. My husband Josh had finished seminary in the spring of 2008 and received a call to his first church. We made the move with our crew from a small town in Michigan to a smaller town in Indiana. When we arrived, the quiet parsonage next to the cornfield suddenly became filled with playthings, noise, and children.

At that time we had four children: Lorraine, the "Other Mother" (age 5); Aggie, the "Party Starter" (almost 4); Seth, the "Inquisitor" (age 2); and Marcus, the "Wild Monkey" (10 months). We hardly had finished unpacking when we found out we were expecting our fifth child. I believe we sighed a little, then shrugged, then smiled. We knew God easily could make room in our hearts and home for one more.

It was a time of abundant, noisy blessings. Five children, age 5 and younger, energetically consumed our food, our time, and our hearts. Things such as free time, organized closets, and short-term memory had become things of the past for this mother. The level of chaos was such that I had difficulty remembering to eat breakfast each day, to make sure the children brushed their teeth, and recalling whose turn it was to ride in the front seat. I woke up tired every day, unable to survive without coffee and prayer. I spent my days feeding, cleaning, and chasing after children; and I went to bed exhausted every night, covered with cracker crumbs, kisses, and boogers. It was a busy life, but a very good one.

cⵯﾟ

I enjoy going to the park with the children. The wide open spaces and climbing contraptions keep them busy and agreeable for long stretches of time. It is also good exercise for me. It is just a short walk from the house, but I generally do a good deal of swing-pushing. If I am feeling ambitious, I will even instigate a tickle-fight. I am typically out of breath for our entire visit, if nothing else, from the constant talking that is part of my daily job. I find it quite challenging to listen and respond to four separate little-people conversations at once.

"Mommy, look at me!"

"Mommy, watch!"

"Mommy, Marcus is on the slide again! He might fall down!"

"AAAAAAAAAAHHHHHH! I hurt myself!"

"Mommy, can you push me?"

"Mommy, remember that time we were here with Grammy?"

"Mommy, can you lift me up on the monkey bars?"

"Mommy, watch!"

"WAAAAA! I hurt myself again! Can you kiss it?"

"Hey, Mommy, look!"

"Mommy, can you do this?"

"Mommy, watch!"

They are diligent little children, always watching for a sign of laziness on their mother's part, ready to go into repeat-and-whine mode should they suspect I am shirking my important job of listening to every word they say.

Though they all are talkers, Aggie is the one who earned the nickname "Jibber Jabber." When she is really on a roll, she will tell you in one breath exactly what she ate for breakfast, what kind of toothpaste she likes best, and what color panties she is wearing. Talking with her often feels like a verbal drive-by shooting.

One beautiful day in the middle of October, we were at the park and the cacophony of noise was going on as usual. I was attempting the impossible: trying to have an adult conversation with my friend, Mary Anne, while also remaining involved in the park-time noise fiesta. Agnes and Marcus were playing together on the slides, laughing and giggling and chasing each other.

All of a sudden, something was not right. Agnes had stopped on the top of the slide, right in the middle of a rambunctious game with Marcus, and she stared off into space. It was as if an enormous silence had taken hold of her. Her expression was completely blank.

"Aggie? Aggie, what are you looking at? Ag?" I asked, walking over to her.

And then she was back, laughing with Marcus and going down the slide as if nothing had happened. *Was it just me or was that weird?* I looked at Mary Anne and could see that she was trying to hide her concern as well. We did not speak of it then.

Her departure was not dramatic, but now I realize, that was the day "normal Aggie" began to go away. Quietly she turned in to a new kind of Aggie, and I became a new kind of mother. The changes were subtle and small, yet each day, relentlessly, changes kept coming.

Aggie is the kind of child who never needs to be asked what she is thinking. If her little voice is not already telling you that and more, all you have to do is look at her eyes. No need for a mood ring—just make eye contact. I remember after she was born, when she was still in the hospital, we noticed her "Aggie scowl." Her grumpy moods are infrequent, but so dramatic they are almost funny. Her ugly feelings create not only a deep crease on her forehead and a frown, but even seem to bring a dark cloud into the room that hovers directly over her head as long as her mood lasts.

Her cheery moods are just as contagious. When she was a baby, even before she could coo, her eyes sparkled with mischievous delight and laughter. Her Grandpa called her "Dancing Eyes," and the name continued to fit her as she got older.

After that first strange incident, I began watching Aggie a little more closely. *Is it just me*, I wondered, *or do her eyes look dark and sunken, as they always do when she is about to get sick?* Every day or two I would notice something that I thought might be an "episode." Every time I would second guess myself afterwards, *Am I being paranoid? Was she just daydreaming?*

I mentioned my worries to Josh and he began watching her, too. Family members said they also noticed some "daydreaming," but none of them thought it was worth mentioning. As the days went on, we noticed that her staring episodes sometimes would include a strange, humorless giggle.

The word "seizure" did not occur to us at first. Like most people, we thought seizures always involved falling and convulsions. We had never heard of "absence seizures" or "complex partial seizures," the kind that manifest with other symptoms, some of which are confused with daydreaming. It took only a few days of Aggie's strange episodes to make me curious enough to search the Internet, and only a cursory glance at a couple of web pages to scare me enough to call the doctor. He said what I then expected: it could be nothing, or it could be seizures. He ordered an EEG and an MRI.

It takes time to schedule major tests, and time for doctors to receive results and pass them on to the family. I do not recall how much time it took exactly, but it was much too long for this mommy. In an effort to do *something* for her while during that awful waiting period I began to keep a journal of her episodes and to research as much as possible.

October 24
    Aggie woke up at 7, normal behavior, happy and energetic, noted sunken eyes.
    9:30 a.m. Aggie asked for a cookie. I said, "OK, but take the bag down to share with the rest of the kids."
    "I want a cookie," she said again.
    "Aggie, you can have one, just take these down to share, OK? Honey, do you understand?"
    She looked at me with an odd smile on her face and said "Yes...no...yes.... no" As she spoke her eyes looked off to the side and she started giggling.
    "Aggie? Aggie, can you take this downstairs, Honey?" I touched her shoulder and she looked at me like she was trying to get her bearings. I explained one more time, and she ran off with the cookies.
    11:30 a.m. Aggie got confused when I gave her direction, began giggling repeatedly (not a belly laugh but almost like she had an inside joke with herself.)
    She slept well in the afternoon: a three hour nap as usual.
    5:30 p.m. We were playing a loud family game and she stopped interacting with me, to watch a fly perhaps? She appeared unable to hear me for a few seconds.

7:45 p.m. I found her wandering aimlessly in her room, confused.

I soon filled pages and pages with details, not knowing whether any of it would be important. Constant observation made me certain of one thing: *something was wrong.* Every day in a hundred ways, I could see it. I worried about it, cried over it, and hated it, as I stared at this problem in my home each day. We had no official diagnosis, so the rest of the family, quite logically, still held out hope and fended off worry fairly easily. But not me. For me, the problem was enormous, and my biggest fear was that the tests would be done and they would not be able to pinpoint the cause. There was an unspoken plea from my heart to everybody I saw: *Something is wrong, please tell me you can see it, too!* It was a plea often followed by a silent prayer, *Please, Jesus, help!*

Slowly the burden of worry began to sink down into my heart. *Something is very, very wrong.* The phrase was not always in my mind, but the feeling began to seep into every one of my interactions with Aggie, and soon it trickled into all of my waking moments.

Chapter 3
Testing Begins

In early November, Aggie had her first test: an EEG. If, indeed, her brain was prone to seizures, sleep deprivation made it more likely that she would have one during the test. We were directed to bring her to the test exhausted, so she was allowed no more than four hours of sleep the night before. Since Aggie was normally such an active little child, we did not think keeping her up would be much of a problem.

Josh and I tried to convince her that it was a good night for a party. "Aggie, you get to have special daddy-time tonight after all the kids go to bed! You can eat Oreos and do whatever you want. Isn't that great?" She was very excited about the Oreos; but after those were eaten, things got a little rough. I think that was about 8:15 p.m. At 9 p.m., she announced that she was ready for bed. Josh tried everything he could think of, even taking her across the backyard to the church's school to play in the gym, but nothing kept her happy for long. By 9:45 p.m., she started crying and begging for sleep. They spent two more hours in misery, and barely made it until midnight.

It was my job to wake her up at 4 a.m. She immediately resumed crying and begging for sleep. After trying to read a book and play with her, I quickly learned that only water-related activities would keep her awake. Poor kid! I don't know how many baths and showers she had by the time it was all over! Despite the fact that she was very, very clean when we left for the test, she still looked like she had slept in the city park that night. The sour expression that began on her face somehow managed to creep into the rest of her body, mess her hair, and wrinkle her clothes. As Josh drove us to the test, I sat next to our scowling Aggie and worked hard to keep her awake.

She was cooperative for the actual test, probably because she was much too tired to put up a fight. She had to sit still while they put 25 electrodes in her hair, secured with nasty, sticky stuff. During the test the technician asked her to blow on a Kleenex, because hyperventilation can also induce seizures in a person who is prone to them. She did this with great enthusiasm, then immediately had an "episode." After that, they told her she could sleep on my lap, and she was snoring in about 30 seconds. We rewarded her with an orange push-up from the gas station, the only ice cream treat we could find so early in the morning.

God is merciful, and so we all got naps before the next appointment of the day—my ultrasound! If you have forgotten that I was pregnant through all of this, know that I often did the same thing. Baby number five, at this stage, was so tiny and so easy to care for that we hardly knew he was there! As the three of us piled back into the car, Josh said, "It is a strange day when the ultrasound is *not* the biggest event of the day!" The ultrasound was on time, painless, and wonderfully uneventful. The baby looked perfectly healthy, and we could even see through our sleep deprived eyes that it was most definitely a boy!

To small children, ultrasound pictures of babies bear little resemblance to real babies. I was hoping for some sweet big-sister reaction when I said, "Aggie, it's a boy!" She just said, "Oh." Later when she looked at the pictures she said skeptically, "It looks like a turtle!"

Despite the unclear pictures, the family was excited, especially big sister Lorraine. Sources say she was grinning from ear to ear when she told her kindergarten class at school. I was excited, too. It is odd how I have become quite comfortable with boys. I never really thought I would be. I had no brothers myself, and, until recently, I did not know the difference between a back hoe and a fork lift. But now I realize that boys are quite simple to understand, at least when they are small. They want mess, machinery, and action! It makes me glad for the wide-open spaces we have here in the country! I can just see myself, opening the back door in the morning and, as the boys run out of the house, I yell, "There's a mud hole boys, and here are some shovels! See you at lunch time!"

After the ultrasound we picked up the boys from our friend's house. I do not know how many times I thanked God for our dear friends during our struggles with Aggie. Other mothers, even those with several children, had such compassion for us and our sick child, they constantly offered help and support. On the day of the EEG, a dear friend not only watched our boys along with her own children all day, she also sent us home with dinner for that night!

That was a good thing, as I consider what I would have done with the last few drops of energy that remained in my exhausted body. I imagine myself staggering into the kitchen, thinking, *Hmmmm, what will fill their stomachs?* I smile as I spy the Halloween candy, reasoning, *That has lots of calories and there is plenty of it!* I grab the enormous bowl, plop it on the dinner table, and shout "dinner's ready!" The kids almost knock me over as they run for the candy, while I stagger towards the couch and fall asleep for the rest of the night.

The next day was recovery day and waiting-by-the-phone day. What I expected to hear was, "Yep, she had a seizure. Here are the next tests she needs and the specialist you have to go to." It is funny how the word "seizure" was so terrifying to me at the very beginning. By the time the

EEG was done, I was almost positive she was, indeed, having seizures. I had decided that the word "seizure" and even the word "epilepsy," while worrisome, were something I could handle.

When the doctor did call with the report, "Aggie had a seizure in her temporal lobe. She has epilepsy," the words produced no tears. In fact, I remember a sense of relief. I finally had a name for that awful sense that *something is wrong*. A diagnosis usually has a corresponding treatment plan, which then would restore health, normalcy, and a sense of control. *So, she might have to take a pill for the rest of her life. It could be worse!*

As time went on, I learned that epilepsy is much more complicated than I imagined. Knowing she was having seizures simply led to more questions: What kind(s) of seizures is she having? And can we find an underlying cause? The answers to those two questions would determine our next step.

Her moments of "silence" continued during those days. Now that we knew she was having seizures, we began to become more and more accustomed to the minor interruptions they caused. Her seizures at this point were typically less than a minute long and seemed to disturb her normal activities only briefly. *Do we even bother with medicine?* I wondered at times. *Is it worth the possible side effects, or do we just learn to live with these interruptions? Maybe she will grow out of it if we give her time.*

The diagnosis seemed to bring more questions than answers, and I soon realized it was the next step that I really feared: investigating the underlying causes. Aggie was scheduled for blood work and an MRI. For several weeks we were in limbo just waiting for tests, waiting for answers, waiting for a treatment plan of some sort.

It seems strange to me that life goes on in times like this. Yet it did. We wrestled in the leaves, I changed diapers and cooked meals, the mom's group came over every Friday, and we all watched my belly grow bigger and bigger. The seizures came and came, disturbing some of Aggie's best moments, but she hardly seemed to notice. As soon as the seizure let her go, she would hop right back into the present moment as if nothing ever happened.

Lord, teach me to do that, too, I begged.

Chapter 4
Gratitude

"As parents you may not realize it, but somewhere along the way you tend to take your children into yourself, as if they were really yours. We forget that our children are, first of all, God's—on loan to us for only a season."

My father-in-law said this one evening as we were discussing Aggie's health problems. The children were all in bed after a cheerful evening wrestling with their grandparents. I sat quietly as Josh explained Aggie's diagnosis to his parents. He was logical and calm as he described the possible futures we could be facing with Aggie, and his parents seemed to receive the information with an equal amount of calmness. Meanwhile, I hugged my pillow and tried to keep the tears back, praying that God would give me faith like these strange people.

I attempted to wrap my mind around that awful idea: *They are on loan to us for a season, not forever.* My heart has always fought this every time I noticed my children growing up. The passing years were forcing me to release them in small ways, but often I would do it unwillingly, and with great sadness for myself. A selfish mother, I was hoping to keep them to myself forever. I was enjoying the simple days with my dear pre-schoolers, having them under my care, in my arms, in my home where I could love and enjoy them. Once again, signs of change were everywhere, but I was trying to turn away. I was not looking forward to the day they would grow wings and leave my nest. I was refusing to admit that their lives, as they flourished, would lead them slowly away from me.

I was having trouble accepting the natural separation of parents and children as they lived life, so naturally, I could hardly comprehend that other potential means of separation that could be in our future: death. As I researched epilepsy and began to genuinely fear for Agnes's life, I became painfully aware of this awful possibility. I realized that God most certainly could take Aggie home to Him at an early age. Even though I only just barely could bring myself to even think of it, I was certain her death would feel like an injustice beyond anything I could imagine. And yet, I would have no ground on which to stand and complain.

Our children are not ours. They are God's. My heart was rebelling violently against this, though it is so obviously true. I may have carried my children, but I certainly did not create them. I could feed them and care for them, but I could not protect them from every evil. My willpower does not cause their hearts to beat each day. Though I would attack epilepsy like an angry mama-bear, I could not force it to let go of my daughter. The grip I had on Aggie was not holding, and it was not helping her get better. I did not possess her, and I had no right to demand to keep her.

Yet somehow, I had to make it through days that contained all of these things I could not control. My fears about Aggie were often like a giant, splattered bug that nearly covered the windshield of my mind, blinding me to everything else. Some days, I let my worries interfere with hundreds of little moments that I could have been enjoying her, making memories with her and the other children, serving and loving those around me. I often would allow fear of the future take hold of my mind. I did not think of my Father who is caring for us today and who has promised to care for us in any kind of future.

Even though it was only beginning, this trial was like a fire to me, burning away my misunderstandings of the world and myself, and exposing the selfishness of my heart. What a blessed relief it was to join the congregation of sinners at church each Sunday, daring with them to stand in God's presence while admitting out loud the ugly truth that we are "sinful and unclean." I brought my scorched heart to God, and He soothed it with the living water, His Word, and His servant faithfully reminded me once again, "God has given his Son to die for you, and for his sake, forgives you all your sins."

Grace, love, mercy, compassion, and forgiveness of sins—Jesus Himself, sustained me even as I continued to wrestle. Unanswered questions remained, even fear and sin remained, but Jesus did not forsake me. His grace helped me sleep at night and mixed with a hundred other blessings to help me make it through the days.

Because my patient Father knew what I needed, He allowed this trial into my life when my house was filled with small children. If I was to learn to live in the present and trust Him with the future, what better teachers could He have sent to me? On the wall of our dining room we had a huge picture of a cornucopia, a teaching tool to remind the children of their blessings as we got ready for Thanksgiving. Each day each child would add a new fruit or vegetable with something written on it for which they were thankful. The simplicity of their gratitude always made me smile.

"Thank you, Jesus, for wrestle time with Daddy."

"Thank you, Jesus, for my snuggly bed."

"Thank you, Jesus, for superman pajamas."

"Thank you, Jesus, for doors."

My kids understood God's care for His children better than I did sometimes. They had the ability to see every little thing in their lives, right down to the buttery pancakes, as blessings directly from the hand of their loving Heavenly Father. They wasted no time wondering whether God was good. They looked around, they saw their blessings, and they knew He could be trusted.

Lord, help me to look around as the children do. Let me see the ways you care for me even in this time of trial. God did open my eyes just as I asked. While the ugly bug-splatter of Aggie's problem was always somewhere in my line of vision, I also began to see the blessings from His hand that were meant to encourage me and help me through the days. A warm bed, a home, food, friends, and air to breathe: God gives all of these little things freely and faithfully, every day, again and again and again. How often I forget that these things are gifts and see them as entitlements! If He even threatens to take one away of His million gifts, I throw a temper tantrum and doubt His goodness toward me.

My heart still threw temper tantrums at times. I tried to tell myself the truth. *My children are not my own, they are on loan only for a season. God loves Aggie more than I do and He knows what He is doing.* Yet my heart still strongly desired some very specific blessings for my Agnes. *I want her to be able to go to school. I want her to be able to ride a bike and drive a car. I want her to reach adulthood. I want to enjoy her for years to come. Lord, forgive me, I don't want You to take her away!* The list of "wants" in my head sometimes became so loud they were all I could think about.

But God is gentle and patient. In the midst of inner turmoil He often sent me simple reminders of His care for me. A meal, a hug, a reason to laugh out loud. He moved my eyes from that ugly bug splatter to the rest of the world, to the ways He cares for me, His child.

> *Thank you for my husband's embrace.*
> *Thank you for this cup of coffee.*
> *Thank you for Marcus's belly laugh.*
> *Thank you God for snuggly warm blankets.*

"O give thanks to the LORD, for He is good, for His steadfast love endures forever." (Psalm 107:1)

Chapter 5
Low and High

The night before Aggie's MRI was not a peaceful one for me. At that point I had been reading too much, and had too many ideas of the future that might be in store for Aggie and our family. During the day, fears and worries assaulted when seizures struck; but our busy home was full of life even during a time of sickness, and usually I was able to focus on the tasks at hand and carry on. Nights were much worse: those images swarmed around my head and invaded my dreams.

The day we went to the children's hospital for the MRI was more like a night to me. Here, the images of sickness and suffering children did not just stay in my head. They were in the waiting rooms with us, in the toy room and in the hallway, and this time, they were real. I saw a child with a blank expression and odd mannerisms. *Had she once been a bouncy four year old like Aggie?* There was another in a wheelchair, and another too sick to sit up. Tired parents were everywhere. This was a club I did not want to join.

Aggie bounced around the waiting room, enjoying the toys and books, talking constantly, and oblivious to everything else. I watched my piggy-tailed little girl entertain herself, amazed that she did not notice the terrified screams of the other kids who were going into the room for IV sedation before her. When it came time for Aggie to have her MRI, Josh and I took her into the dimly lit room, where the nurses attempted to joke with her to put her at ease. The room was dark, sterile, and ominous. Even Aggie could tell that it was no place for humor.

When they began to put in the IV, Josh and I held her and tried to comfort her. She screamed for all she was worth, and cried so hard one would think they were sawing off her arm. "When will it be over, mommy?" she asked as I tried to soothe her with her teddy bear blanket and hold her still at the same time. Her screams continued without an answer, and as I looked into her terrified eyes and stroked her hair, the nightmarish images of suffering began to fill my head. *Would this be the first of many painful trips to the hospital for my sweet baby? Will there come a day after chemotherapy, radiation, and a million other horrors when my little child will scoff at an IV poke?* Despite my best efforts, my tears fell and mixed with hers.

As I tried to focus all of my energies on keeping her still and praying that they would get the IV done, she did something I will never forget. For a brief second, she completely stopped her screams and crying, caught my eye with hers, and asked with genuine hope, "Mommy, can we go home now?"

There I was holding her down, actually forcing her to undergo this needle torture, and she asked me this. She had no understanding of what is going on, only that they were hurting her, and Mommy and Daddy were forcing her to stay put. Yet she *still* had hope that we would make it go away. Of course, I wanted with all my heart to say yes to her, beat up the nurses, and whisk her off to our home where we would read books under blankets all day and forget this ever happened; but I could not.

Eventually the IV was in place, the medicine kicked in, and sleep overcame her rebellion. They wheeled Aggie and her teddy bear blanket away, and I was glad she was finally at peace. For the sake of the baby I carried, I could not be with my other baby during her MRI, so I left her with the staff and her daddy. During the test I wandered the hospital looking for somewhere to have a hearty meltdown. My knees were shaking as I wandered through the halls until I found a quiet place.

Finally, away by myself in the hospital chapel, I sat down and could do nothing but cry. For several minutes it was just tears—no words, no thoughts, only an enormous wave of grief and fear that simply washed over me. *Oh, Jesus, I can't bear it. I can't watch my child suffer and maybe even die in front of me. Oh, Jesus, can't you just come back, today, right now, before I have to hear the awful news that my daughter has a brain tumor? I can't make it through that valley, Lord, can't you just whisk us away to the end of the story?*

I realized that like her, I was writhing in pain, and somehow, "Daddy, can we go home now?" was all I could pray.

His silence told me, "No," and it gave me no explanation why.

Because I could not hide in that chapel forever, eventually I gave myself a little pep talk. *OK, you don't even know anything yet. Right now all you have to bear is what is in front of you. You had to bear that awful IV poke, now that is over. Now you have to bear waiting for the test, and that is all. After that you will have to get her and take her home. Tomorrow you will have to bear waiting for the phone to ring, and then you will have to bear the results. One thing at a time. Just breathe.*

The waves of grief calmed down a little bit and I began to catch my breath again. My next prayer was quiet and simple, *Lord, please, give me the strength to walk out of this chapel and face the next thing.*

Though I wanted to find a way to free myself from the pain, to "quit" even at this early stage, I did not. I would have, had I been left alone. But God did hear my prayer,

Emily Cook

and He gave me the strength for the next step. He took my shaking hands and reminded me that all I had to do was to focus on what was in front of me, and when even that was too much, He was right there to help me.

His help enabled me to leave the chapel and return to the waiting room. God gave strength to my knees and helped me hold back my tears for a time. As I walked the halls of the hospital I was conscious of how horrible I looked with my red eyes and red nose. The ache in my heart became greater and my prayers even more fervent as I realized we were just one of many suffering families in this awful place. *Lord, have mercy.* I walked faster, my arms suddenly aching to hold my little girl again.

Soon Aggie was done with her test. I walked into the room where she was groggily stirring under her teddy bear blanket. She lay on the hospital bed, still clinging to sleep, content not to remember the IV battle or why she was there. She may have been at peace, but Josh and I could not help but interrupt her sleep as soon as we could, encouraging her to wake up and drink something, so they would let us get out of that hospital.

❧

As we left the radiology department, I carried her belongings and tried to hold her hand, grateful to be close to her and have that ordeal behind us. Aggie was not interested in holding my hand. She wanted to run down the halls ahead of us, and though she kept falling, she refused to be convinced that she needed help. The anesthesia that was still in her system made her act almost like she was inebriated. She was giggly, forgetful, and just plain silly. As we tried to keep her from hurting herself, we could not help but laugh along with her.

- 26 -

As we waited for a copy of her medical records, we gave her some candy. She attempted to toss some in her mouth, missed completely, and sent them rolling on to the floor. She jumped up to get them, wobbling and staggering in the general direction of the candy. She and I were both giggling as I grabbed her, and she was easily distracted with another piece of candy from my pocket. Despite her protests, Josh carried her the rest of the way to the car so she would not hurt herself.

We took her out to Bob Evans for pancakes on the way home. In hindsight, I am not sure how wise it was to take a tipsy four-year-old out in public, but it certainly was an adventure! Aggie's voice had no volume control, and so the waitress, along with the entire restaurant, soon knew that she wanted some "CHOCOLATE MILK and PANCAKES.... and SYRUP...and A PLATE, TOO!"

As Josh and I watched her dip her pancakes and put them in her mouth (or thereabouts,) we gave up the hope of an enjoyable meal out. Instead, we sought only to minimize the damage and get out of there as quickly as possible. She seemed to have lost any kind of social awareness. She got a thought in her head and immediately acted on it. The words "I need the syrup" never made it to her lips, but as soon as she thought it, she was reaching for the syrup, and if she could not reach, she simply climbed on the table! Josh said, "It's like Aggie without inhibitions!" I never really thought she had inhibitions, but compared to tipsy Aggie, I guess she actually did use a great deal of self-control on a normal day!

All the way home she talked and laughed about everything she saw. "Look a ladder! Laaaaddeerrr...ladderladder laaaader...that's a silly word!" When she ran out of funny words to say, she would remember her brothers, and holler up to us in the front seat, "We can't forget to pick up the boys!" She reminded us, loudly, at least twenty times. Then she would look out the window and smile to herself, saying "I love my brothers. I LOOOVE Seth. I LOOOVE Marcus!"

When we finally got home, her antics were becoming less amusing. The other children were glad to see her at first and giggled and wrestled right along with her for awhile, but even they were not sure they wanted all-out wrestling matches for the rest of the day. We attempted to watch a movie as a family, but we really just watched Aggie. After we all got sick of saying "Aggie, quit it! Aggie, sit down! Aggie, I don't want to wrestle! Aggie, put that down! Aggie, quit wiggling! Aggie sit DOWN!" we gave up and went to bed. Exhaustion won out over worry that night, and we all slept well.

Chapter 6
Keep Moving

The next day Aggie still was wild. She woke up early, going at full speed, and spent the first two hours of the day dropping stuff, running people over, hurting her family and herself, and basically creating chaos in every part of the house. Just when I was pulling my hair out and thinking, *Why can't it be summer so she can go outside?* a friend called and offered to have my kids over to play with hers for the afternoon. I laughed and said "You are a brave woman! If you and your kids are ready for chaos, then absolutely, yes!"

Once again, God knew exactly what I needed to make it through that day: a few hours alone. The house was quiet, but my mind was nowhere near peaceful as I awaited the phone call with the results of the MRI. Nervous energy was bursting out of me. So while the children were gone, I power-cleaned, researched epilepsy, snacked, paid bills, and snacked some more. And I think I prayed, too, though sometimes I have trouble stopping my restless activities to actually get the words out. Because of the stress of that day, distraction seemed to be the only way to keep my fragile self from falling apart. I feared that if I stopped to look the PROBLEM in the face, even to bring it to the Lord, I would breakdown completely. So, I simply let my mind and my hands run from one thing to another. I cannot say I found much peace that way, but I found plenty of dust and clutter to look after.

I carried the phone with me to every room as I cleaned. I even stopped to look at it every few minutes, just to make sure it was on and working. After hours of this ridiculous behavior, it finally rang. I took a deep breath as I answered the phone. I knew the stress would make it difficult for me to remember the details of the conversation, so I scrambled to find a pen and paper while I spoke with the doctor. I found a crayon and the inside cover of a coloring book. Close enough.

It turned out to be more inconclusive information. I was desperate for the obvious problem that would lead to the obvious solution, but instead, I was given mere clues. Aggie's MRI showed a little "spot" in her right parietal lobe. As her pediatrician explained, the spot may or may not be the cause of her problems. In fact, he said it is quite common to see a small spot on an MRI done for other reasons. It could be just an abnormality (dysplasia) from when she developed in the womb, scar tissue from a minor infection we never knew she had, or a low grade tumor. We were scheduled to meet with a neurologist the next week.

As the words, "Aggie might have a brain tumor" had been screaming themselves loudly in my head for a couple weeks now, this report did not really change much in my own mind. I passed the information on to family and friends, interpreting the scribbled crayon marks, "more wait and see, not much to report." Although I was not upset about the report, I still cringed inwardly every time I said the words "...or it could be a tumor." I constantly had to remind myself we knew nothing conclusive yet, just take one thing at a time. In other words, *Don't panic!*

Throughout the rest of that week and through the weekend, I watched Aggie play normally, stop to have a seizure, play some more, seize some more, over and over and over. The stretches of normalcy were always short, a few hours at the most. They were much too short to let me actually forget that she was having serious problems. The time ticked by slowly as we waited for her appointment with the neurologist. I was counting down the days to that appointment, to some concrete information, and, *please God,* a treatment plan.

Josh and I spoke with the other children about her seizures, now that we were sure that was the word for those "episodes." The younger children did not really understand what was going on, but Lorraine, our five year old, was quite concerned. She and Aggie are only nineteen months apart, and they are very close friends. Their personalities are quite different, however. While Lorraine might prefer playing dress up and painting pictures of flowers, Aggie would rather pretend she is Peter Pan or wrestle. They worked out their differences easily, and, when Lorraine was not at school, ended up playing together more often than not. Lorraine was keenly aware that Aggie was having some strange problems. Josh and I did our best to admit the obvious problem while at the same time making it seem as small and inconsequential as possible. "Aggie's episodes are called seizures. If you see her have one, please tell Mom or Dad so we can write it down and tell the doctor." Lorraine took this job very seriously. I often heard her holler from another room, "Aggie's having an episode!" Sometimes she would come to tell me after the fact, describing and acting out every little detail.

One day, the girls were in the basement, enjoying a strange combination of dress-up and demolition derby on their bikes. The boys and I were playing with the train set in the living room. It is not easy to set out the train with Marcus around, but it is even harder to keep him away if he knows big brother is playing with it. I was attempting to keep them both happy. Seth and I took turns fending off Marcus's attempts at total destruction of the train village, and we finally got the train working. When he saw the train actually going around the tracks, Marcus finally understood why we kept telling him to stop, sit down, and quit breaking the tracks. He waited an entire three minutes before tromping through the tracks once again.

"Marcus!!!" whined Seth, "get off the tracks!"

Before I could break up the wrestling match, Lorraine came running into the room. "Mommy! Mommy! Aggie just had an episode! We were riding our bikes around and around and then she stopped and looked at the wall like this..." Lorraine made a blank face and continued, "and I said, 'Aggie? Aggie?' And she kept looking like this...and I said, 'Aggie, are you ok?' And she kept looking like this... and then she went, 'huh huh huh...'" Lorraine tried to imitate Aggie's humorless giggle, "and then she got up and started putting on dress up clothes, and she wouldn't talk to me." As Lorraine was talking Aggie came up the stairs wearing a fancy dress, three necklaces, one high heel, and a vacant expression.

"Aggie, Honey, how are you doing?" I asked.

"Pretty good." she said quietly, looking a little confused.

"Honey, are you done riding bikes? Maybe you'd like to sit down and take a rest."

"OK, Mommy." she said. *Wow, that idea is never received so easily,* I thought. I covered her up on the couch and gave her a book to read. She sat with the blanket and the book and looked vaguely towards the boys who were still playing with the train set.

"You're ok, Honey," I said, more to comfort myself than Aggie. "You just had a seizure, that's all. Your body just needs a little quiet time now." I remembered Lorraine, standing there watching us with big worried eyes. "She's fine, Rainy, thank you for telling me."

"OK, Mom. Can I play with the train too?"

"Sure," I said. She got down on the floor with the boys, and I sat next to Aggie. *She's fine now, she's fine.* I held her close and stroked her hair. The seizure was over, but I knew she was far from fine. Those familiar, ugly words flooded my brain once again: *tumor, seizures, brain abnormality, mind altering drugs, epilepsy.* As my mind drifted off I joined Aggie, staring blankly in the general direction of the other children, noticing nothing but my own thoughts.

"Mommy! Marcus keeps stepping on the TRAIN TRACK! MOMMY!!!"

I snapped out of my thoughts and back to reality. "MARCUS!" I yelled. Then I took a deep breath and struggled to keep my feelings out of my voice. "OK, Markie, that's enough train time for you. Why don't you help me make lunch?" At the mention of food he jumped up as he always does, and we went off to the kitchen. The train happily returned to the tracks and Aggie remained quiet on the couch. *Be strong. One thing at a time. Make lunch. Keep moving.* And my favorite encouraging thought: *It is almost naptime.*

Chapter 7
Burdens

Though I worried about Aggie constantly, I attempted to keep the family going as usual. The demands of four kids and one on the way do not let up simply because Mommy has a lot on her mind. Aggie's moments of strange silence were truly only brief moments; the rest of the day was noisy and wild and messy as always.

I had a vague picture of what life was going to be like as a pastor's wife. I intended to jump into church work with both feet, working alongside my husband as often as possible. When we moved to our new home, I had my eyes open for programs that needed starting, for old people who needed visiting, and for children who needed baby-sitting. Sure, I had a few kids myself, but I expected life to be a little easier after the move because I no longer had to work outside the home. *Just let me know where you want me to focus my energies, Lord, and I'm ready!*

My vocation that year turned out to be absolutely nothing like I expected. While I did begin a study group for mothers, I spent the first few months just getting settled and helping the kids get their bearings in our new home. I never anticipated how the workload inside my own home would increase with Aggie's health problems. When things began to change that fall, I changed too, from an energetic, eager-to-help pastor's wife to an exhausted, stressed-out mommy who barely managed to keep up with the demands of her own children.

The days were fairly normal for the children that autumn, but they were lived under a shadow of worry for me. Worry may have consumed me even at this early stage had I not been blessed with so much work to do. I often would catch myself staring off into space even surrounded by the noise of the children, my mind wandering away with questions and concerns about the future mixed with prayer and grief. Those were heavy thoughts to be carrying around while surrounded by children, and I was not always happy to be pulled from them in order to look at a pretty picture or break up a fight. But, God knew I needed the distraction of hard work at that time, and so in His mercy, He kept me very busy during those days. If I was awake, I was working, my feet and hands easily finding something in reach that needed to be done. Stewing in worry is fruitless, if it is done sitting down, but pouring worry into housework felt incredibly productive.

Distraction is helpful up to a point, but no matter how hard I worked, thoughts and fears would break through and force me to acknowledge them. I recall one particular day, when craft time and book time and snack time all were interrupted by seizures. After one of them, Aggie wanted a hug and some "mommy snuggles" while she watched TV. I held her close to me, kissed her hair, and whispered "Jesus, please help Aggie."

"Why did you say that Mommy?" she said, locking her dark and sunken eyes with mine. I was amazed that such sick looking eyes could retain such clueless innocence.

I willed the tears that were forming in my eyes to stay there while I rubbed her back and told her not to worry, that she just seemed tired and maybe her body is fighting something. She was completely unaware that she was having problems at all. Her seizures left absolutely no trace in her memory. She was still my little hummingbird, fluttering around enjoying as much of life as possible. She knew nothing about her parent's worries, the tests that were coming, or the decisions we would have to make for her. She did not know her eyes looked dark and tired, nor why everyone asked her whether she felt okay several times a day.

That night I thought of our friends from college whose first child was a beautiful, premature, very sick little girl. Her parents spent six months in a hospital, and endured days of worry, tests, decisions, and nights of watching and wondering. It hurt them to love her, and it hurt everyone who knew them to watch the entire family suffer. I remember wondering how hard it would be to hold a child attached to so many tubes and wires.

I remember being amazed that her parents' hearts continued to beat even when hers finally stopped, less than six months after she was born. I do not know what baby Vivian knew of the pain, but I am confident that she knew she was loved. Her parents loved her while they bore for her a burden she did not even know she had. They did it with difficulty, but they did it faithfully, with God's help. Every needle poke, every tiny tragedy she suffered, she suffered in her parents arms, wrapped tightly in their love.

And then there was my little Aggie, carrying around epilepsy, a burden that she did not even realize that she had. I saw in the example of my dear friends the clear job of a parent with a sick child: *You must love her.* I always knew this was a mother's job, but with four healthy children, love always had poured out of me easily and naturally. The sacrifice of love was small then, the rewards were tremendous. Suddenly, love began to burn. I was startled by the degree of pain mixed in with my love for Aggie. As seizures continued to assault my daughter and my own heart, I tried to bear her burdens for her, but my own love was utterly insufficient.

Lord, unless you care for Aggie, we test and research and fight for her in vain. But You do care for Aggie. You have promised in her Baptism and in Your Word. She is Your little lamb, Your dear child, and You love her even more than her parents do. You bore her heaviest burden: sin and death. You know how to care when it hurts. You did it when it cost You Your life. You have not promised your children a life without suffering, but you do promise to work all things, even epilepsy, for the good of Your children. Hold Aggie and this family close to You, and sustain us with Your love and Your certain promises.

It hurt terribly to share the burden of epilepsy with Aggie. Everyday moments became colored with both love and pain. The ugly silence of seizures continued to invade our normal days, and love itself began to feel like sickness. Even the bright moments began to burn—her smile, a giggle, fleeting moments of joy—as I feared for her future. My heart writhed in pain while holding her after a seizure, knowing I could do nothing to prevent the next one. Aggie and I were the same in that way: we were small, fragile, and powerless over the future. What could we do but reach out for our Father's arms?

"Blessed be the Lord, who daily bears us up; God is our salvation." (Psalm 68:19)

Chapter 8
Weak and Loved

The weekend before Aggie's appointment with the neurologist, I spent much of my time merely trying to hold myself together. Josh and I were hoping the specialist would be able to give us more information about the spot they found on her brain, and have some sort of strategy for managing her seizures. I imagined every kind of treatment plan, from "Let's just leave her alone and see whether she grows out of it," to "Let's give her some mind-altering drugs and see what happens," to "Let's rush her into surgery immediately!"

Aggie's sunken eyes had become the norm. Though she had unpredictable energy bursts, overall she was significantly more mellow and tired. I had begun to notice a rough pattern in her seizures. Generally, she would have one within ten minutes of waking up, then roughly three more throughout the morning. Typically, she took a three to four hour nap, had another seizure upon waking, and probably at least two more before bed in the evening. She had an average of five to seven seizures per day.

Every few days we noticed another strange, new detail. Some of her seizures were still simply the "daydreaming" kind, others had become more complicated. Sometimes during a seizure she would look off into the distance and laugh at nothing, with an eerie, humorless giggle. During other seizures she would mumble, repeat a phrase or a sound, or even sing. Sometimes she would wander aimlessly during the seizure. After the seizure she might jump right back into whatever she was doing without missing a beat, or she might be confused and tired for an hour or more. It had become completely impossible to predict how Aggie was going to feel from one hour to the next.

As a mother of four young children with one more on the way, I already had been forced to learn how to be flexible. In some respects, chaos is easy for me to tolerate. I am not bothered by loud music, mismatched socks, or unmade beds. But when chaos messes up my to-do list or my plans for the day, I feel very unsettled. It is impossible to predict when I might need to call the poison control center, clean up after a stomach bug, or take a visit to the Emergency Room. This is simply life with small children, and I was learning to live with that. I was making much shorter lists than I did before we had children, and I tried to have only vague ideas of when each thing might be accomplished.

The children also were learning to be flexible in their own ways, an important skill for survival in a large family. Like her mother, Aggie did not give much thought to what she wore. We approached our closets looking for something handy and comfortable. If it matched, it was usually luck. Seth, on the other hand, was very conscious of his appearance. He most certainly did not appreciate mismatched clothing, including pajamas. He actually would notice if he put his clothes on backwards. He would loudly remind me to put his pillow on his bed right-side up. I could hardly believe he noticed such things, so I would try to trick him. Without fail, he would scold me, "Mommy! That's not the right way!"

As he flipped over the pillow, I would smile and ask, "Are you sure, Honey? I think the wheels are supposed to go on the top."

"No, Mommy!" His laugh carried a touch of panic as he adamantly flipped it over, "It goes like this!" He plopped his head down on the pillow, hard, hoping I would leave it the RIGHT way. I suspect I drove him nuts with my flexibility in some areas. He would not only notice, but even complain if I left the top of the syrup open, even if I was just going to use it again in a few minutes. On occasion he would follow me as I worked around the house, assuming the job of closing cupboards and drawers after me. "Are you done with that yet, Mama? Can I close it?"

While I have never shared my son's sense of order, my flexibility also has its limits. Unpredictability that comes naturally with young children is one thing, and a real challenge in its own right, but the unpredictability that seizures brought into our lives was exponentially more difficult to manage. *Will we be going to church this Sunday? Can we go to the grocery store? Can Aggie follow basic directions like "go put away your shoes?" Can she play with other children?* The answers to these questions varied drastically depending on when, how often, and what kind of seizures Aggie was having on any particular day.

Five to seven times each day my heart sank as I watched her suffer a seizure. Yet, so many other times, she would seem absolutely fine, life and health bursting out of her as if she'd never been sick at all. *See, she's fine. No, she's not. She's really sick. Oh, come on, she's really not that bad. Yes, she is. No, she isn't.* Back and forth I went in my head, my heart desperate and hopeful and grieving all at once.

I tried to be strong, to put a wall around those thoughts and feelings, at least during the day when I was surrounded by my family. Yet the mere frequency of her seizures made that impossible. Somehow I had to find a way to function even with all these thoughts and feelings going on inside me. I had no idea how to do that.

That weekend I got an email from my Aunt Julie. Like many other friends and family, she wrote to encourage us and promise prayers for the family. She gave me some heartfelt advice she had gained while raising her daughter with Down's Syndrome. After sharing words of sympathy and encouragement, she ended her email saying, "People tell you to be strong—I say be weak and be loved."

I sat at my computer and cried, finally giving myself permission to feel those awful feelings I had been trying to keep at bay. My heart poured out complaints and prayers to God, as I admitted I most certainly was not strong, as I wanted to be. *Lord, I am weak, much too weak for this trial. If there is going to be any strength, it is going to have to come from You.*

Part of me wishes I could describe how I became superwoman from that point on, valiantly facing every obstacle and soldiering on with courage and strength until I found help for my dear daughter. No, I was still weak. My head and my heart still hurt. My problems did not disappear. But I was weak *and loved*. My aunt's words reminded me of that important truth, and I sat at my computer, drenched in tears, and just rested in that word. *Loved.*

The next morning we got up for church. It was a struggle for this weary mother. I knew I needed the gifts that God offers at church, but I also knew that receiving those gifts required getting out of bed, getting dressed, dressing children, and going out in public. It required effort, and worst of all, social interaction. It required putting on makeup and a cheerful-looking face.

Our new church family was incredibly close-knit. Nobody was in a hurry to get anywhere, and yet somehow news always traveled quickly. Not only did everyone know their neighbors, but they likely were related somewhere down the line. As one of the members explained, "We are like one big, big, BIG family 'round here!" It seemed like almost every day someone would drop off some fresh produce for the family, or stop by to offer tractor rides for the children. It took just a few fiddle-playing, pie-baking acts of kindness to make it obvious that we were welcomed. We were loved right into the family.

When the storm began to hit, at first I was tempted to try to hide away and bear it alone, if possible. I was not comfortable sharing burdens and tears with an entire community of "extended family," who despite their kindnesses, still were strangers. Though I wanted to be, I was not the active pastor's wife who worked alongside her husband, serving the church with both hands. Handicapped as I was, I just did not know how I was to relate to church people. Do I actually let them see our need?

As I got the children ready for church early that morning, I was fragile, impatient, and wondering whether we should bother going. We made it somehow, though I was not feeling very kind towards my children or grateful towards God for much that day. I was not handling any of it well. I was still weak, but little did I know that I was about to "be weak and loved" right there in front of everybody.

Marcus was finally settled in the nursery, I had answered all the "How's Aggie?" questions that I could, and I was settled in the pew with the three older children. As He often does, God used my husband to speak words of comfort to me that day. In his sermon, Josh spoke to the church about his own weakness and pain watching Aggie struggle. He read the Word of God: "'I myself will be the shepherd of my sheep, and I myself will make them lie down, declares the Lord GOD. 'I will seek the lost, and I will bring back the strayed, and I will bind up the injured, and I will strengthen the weak..."' (Ezekiel 34:15-16a)

Once again there it was: assurance that God loves the weak. He was not surprised that I was having so much difficulty carrying out His simple command to love. He was not surprised to look at my heart and see that it was weak, and yet He loved me. Not only does He love the weak, He seeks them out and cares for them—even me, a mommy whose faith is too weak to trust God with the future, whose heart is too weak to bear a little epilepsy.

It was a Sunday of shared tears and tissues, as so many bore our burden with us that day. Others had their own reasons for grief and tears and weakness. What a blessing it was to join with all those weak people that day, to admit our need together, and to receive strength from our God who cares for the weak. Together we prayed, "Lord, have mercy;" and He always does.

Jesus, Lover of my soul,
Let me to Thy bosom fly
While the nearer waters roll,
While the tempest still is high.
Hide me, O my Savior, hide,
Till the storm of life is past;
Safe into the haven guide.
Oh, receive my soul at last![2]

Chapter 9
A Treatment Plan

Encouraged by the love of family, church family, friends, and God himself, Josh, Aggie and I left for our appointment with the neurologist. Aggie's most pressing question, "Will I have to get a shot?" had been answered to her satisfaction, so she played contentedly in the car as we drove to Indianapolis. I actually did get some sleep the night before, which was more evidence to me that God did hear and answer prayer. Though I did have a small knot in my stomach, I was functioning. He was carrying me.

Dear Father, thank You for Your constant provision for Aggie and her family. As we go to meet with her doctor this morning, help us to remember that she is Your child, and You love her more than we do. Help us to trust You no matter what we face today, knowing that You have promised never to forsake Your children and to bring good out of every evil we face in this life. You have promised peace for Your children even in the most difficult situations. Please graciously grant this peace to her parents and all who are concerned for her. Thank You for Your great love for us. Amen.

The neurologist's office was a place of sadness like the children's hospital, and we waited alongside other children with various brain problems. Aggie and I took turns drawing pictures back and forth on her Hello Kitty white board. As she copied every picture I did, she could not refrain from adding her own amusing touches. "Look, Mommy, this is you and Daddy.... and Daddy is wearing a dress!" She giggled. That day it was her job to keep her mother occupied in the waiting room during those long minutes before the appointment, and she did her job well.

To my great relief, Aggie's doctor was someone I trusted immediately. His demeanor assured me of his experience and knowledge, and he also showed compassion and care for Aggie. It takes a special talent to be able to discuss the details of brain chemistry with worried parents while also making friends with an active, goofy four-year-old!

Based on Aggie's EEG, the neurologist confirmed that Aggie had been experiencing complex-partial seizures. The spot that showed up on her MRI may or may not be the culprit. He was not able to determine what exactly it was (displaysia, scar tissue, or a low-grade tumor). She would have to have another MRI in three months to find out whether whatever-it-was grew or changed at all. Regardless of what it was, it was small enough that the first line of attack was obvious to the doctor: medication to treat the seizures. "Seventy percent of people diagnosed with epilepsy are able to control seizures with medication." he explained. "Our goal is to find the right medicine and the right dosage to make her seizure free and side-effect free." My, that sounded nice, and he said it with such confidence, I was beginning to hope it was possible. "This may be a rough road of trial and error," he cautioned, as he wrote out her prescription.

So maybe there was not to be a quick fix, but at least now we had something to try. I took a deep breath as I read the potential side effects. *How would you be able to tell if a four-year-old was having suicidal thoughts?* I wondered. As scary as the risks were, we had no choice but to give it a try. By this time, her seizures were coming so often and changing her in such ways that we knew we could not simply hope that she would grow out of it.

I left the appointment reassured on many levels. I was grateful to find a doctor who seemed both knowledgeable and compassionate, who was worthy of our trust. I was reassured that the "spot" on her brain was not a fast-growing tumor, if it was a tumor at all, and it was in a reachable part of her brain should surgery become necessary down the road. My mind made a quick note of that and then shoved the word "surgery" as far away from my thoughts as it could, pretending "down the road" was at least ten years away, down a road we probably never would have to travel. I held on to those sweet words, "seizure free, side effect free," and prayed that Aggie's help would come quickly, through medicine, through this medicine. *This week please.*

Aggie was not excited about her new medicine. She knew we were picking up medicine for her at the pharmacy that afternoon, but she did not need her first dose until that evening. Though I do not recall ever having to give her bad-tasting medicine in the past, she was horribly worried about it. Every few minutes she would whine, "Do I have to take my medicine now? I don't like medicine!"

"No, Honey, you don't need it until bedtime."

A few minutes passed, then, "Is it going to be yucky? I don't want yucky medicine!"

"It will be fine, Aggie, and you don't even need to have it yet."

Ten minutes later, in tears, "I don't like medicine, do I really have to take it now?" After about three hours of this, she had almost made herself sick with worry. We decided to get that first dose over with a little early so she could stop thinking about it.

The next morning she woke up worrying again. Then, as she was bringing her medicine to me, wailing all the way down the hall, somehow she shot a dose of it directly into her eye! *Really dear, taking a little dose of medicine is no big deal, but you know how to make it into a very big deal! I guess the girl who makes all mildly fun moments into a party is also capable of making mildly difficult moments into a tragedy!*

Each dose got a little easier for Aggie. After a few days of watching her like a hawk and seeing no nasty side effects, each dose got a little easier for me, too. After a week we saw no changes in her seizures, but the doctor said it could take up to two weeks to reach the desired level in her brain. So we watched, and we waited, and we continued to live with seizures.

Chapter 10
Seizure Antenna

It continued to get cooler, and before we knew it, the holidays were upon us. For a long time it seemed that Aggie's medicine was doing nothing. There were no side effects, but also no change in seizures. The doctor adjusted the dosage, we watched and waited. Nothing. He adjusted the dosage again. Nothing. During those weeks I developed what I call a "seizure antenna." No matter where we were or what we were doing, one part of my attention was pointed towards Aggie, waiting for that next seizure. I learned to listen for certain types of strange noises (the humorless giggle and so forth), and even if she was in another room I often "picked up" a seizure by noticing a certain kind of silence that seemed out of place. I watched diligently, ready to intervene if needed to keep her safe, recording everything in my journal, and always hoping to spot a reason to believe the medicine was helping.

We still went to the park. I took the children in defiance and anxiety, refusing to allow seizures to keep us hiding in a carpeted room every day. While the children did not realize anything had changed, the entire dynamic for me was new and stressful. My seizure antenna was on "high" if Aggie was climbing, or swinging, or at the top of a slide. If she was out of my sight for a moment, I was restless and inevitably wandered away to check on her. I was constantly trying to evaluate whether "letting her be a kid" was important enough to let her take risks. But my little Aggie wanted so badly to just be a kid! She was the kid on the playground getting all the other kids to have more fun, to run faster, to swing higher; at least, until a seizure came.

I remember one particular day, an exceptionally beautiful day in December, when my children and I joined our friends at the playground. As mothers of large, rambunctious families, my friend and I enjoyed regaining sanity together even as our children swirled around us. We often would get our children together knowing their wildness would increase exponentially when they saw each other, hoping a few hours of wild play would wear them all out.

The children had been having a wonderful time smashing into each other on the twisty slide, but the game of bumper train soon was interrupted by a seizure. I sat in the rocks and the leaves and held Aggie, grateful it happened while she was on the ground and not on the stairs. She looked up, off into the distance, and the seizure washed over her quickly. When it let go of her, she was extremely tired, so I stayed there on the ground with her as she recovered. It had happened quickly and quietly, so the other children noticed no reason to stop their play. They continued to run past us and around us, laughing and wrestling and enjoying the last moments of the setting sun. Only a moment ago Aggie had been in the middle of the fun, but now she was too tired to get up again. She sat quietly on my lap and had nothing to say. The usual shouts of "Look at me, Mommy!" "Push me, Mommy!" "Watch me on the monkey bars, Mommy!" flew happily through the air as always, as the other children continued to play, but my heart was tired and quiet like Aggie's. I had nothing to say, and I knew the other children did not understand why.

Having a seizure antenna was exhausting. When it was on, and it was always on, I was never giving anything else my full attention. I carried concern for Aggie at all times, and I carried a vague sense of guilt towards the healthy children.

I did not like having to run away from a good game of kick-ball with Lorraine to go check on Aggie. I hated making all the kids leave the playground because Aggie was tired, or because my nerves simply could not handle it any more.

When I spoke with friends at church or on the phone, I was always wrestling with inner conflict. Sometimes I felt uneasy because the conversation was distracting me from my important job of watching over Aggie. Often I felt resentful that I even had to have that other job of worrying about Aggie, while other mothers could actually relax while their children were occupied. At other times I felt sorry that I was not fully paying attention to other adults because of the powerful seizure antenna in my head. Or, if I accidentally did give something else my full attention, I would realize it suddenly and become flooded with Aggie panic. *Where is she? Is she OK?*

I was overwhelmed, anxious, sad, and edgy, and at times teetering on the edge of depression. Yet Christmas was coming, with all its glitter and bells and traditions. Before everything changed, I had big plans for sweet memories I wanted to make with the children this year; but how could I, when things had become so difficult? Sinking into some sort of pity party would be much easier, much less exhausting than trying to contrive Christmas joy when I felt so little.

Eventually I found the ambition to lug out the boxes of Christmas decorations. As soon as I did, my children became the teachers and I the student. Sure, they knew our family was having a hard time. Aggie knew she was having seizures now, and the other kids felt my stress and saw my occasionally teary eyes. Yet they seemed incapable of anxiety, innocent of the weight of worry, especially with all those boxes of glittery things at their feet.

Lorraine pulled out a huge, disheveled angel from one of the boxes. "Oh, Mommy," she squealed, "remember this pretty angel? Can I have it in my bedroom again so I can watch her wings change colors while I fall asleep? Can I, can I, please?" Aggie took the cue and began jumping alongside her sister, begging and pleading.

"Sure," I laughed, and the girls ran off with it. Aggie's feet came pounding towards me a second later, Lorraine close behind, so they could tear into the rest of the Christmas treasures. As they did, they squealed and remembered and pestered me to recreate Christmas memories with them.

"Mommy, remember when we sat on the floor by the Christmas tree with all the lights off and read Christmas stories? Can we do that again, Mommy? Can we do it right now?"

"Mommy, remember Christmas lights? OOOH, can we put some in our room again this year? Can you hang them up now?"

"Mommy, can we make cookies and bring them to people again?" "Yeah, cookies! I want a cookie! I want a chocolate chip cookie!" "Me too!" "Me too!" the boys chimed in.

Enthusiasm filled up our house until it was fogging up the windows, and despite myself, I breathed in some of their joy. How could I wait until things were back to "normal" to make memories with the children? They don't seem to need "normal" to enjoy the holiday. *Lord, make me more like my children. Teach me how to live with this seizure antenna and still rejoice.*

Chapter 11
Holiday Dissonance

Later that week I took Lorraine Christmas shopping in the evening. She "ooh'd" and "aah'd" about every light and Santa and Christmas tree. It was a rare treat for me to spend time with one of the healthy children all alone, and I was really enjoying it. We skipped in and out of five stores buying baking supplies and gifts, just the two of us. We had plans to make baked goods for just about every single person we knew. Lorraine even convinced me to buy her a Santa hat, which she vowed to wear all week long.

As we pulled into the parking lot of Hobby Lobby, her "most favorite, favorite store," I got a call from Josh who was at home with the other kids. He told me that Aggie had a seizure while climbing on the bunk bed and fell straight back from the top. She was still having the seizure after she fell, so for several minutes she just laid on the floor unaware of any pain at all. Both of the little boys knew something was very wrong, and as she lay there, they were pacing around her making a fuss. It took about half an hour for her to really notice her aches and pains, and she spent the rest of the night snuggling Daddy on the couch. As Josh and I talked about this new incident, the familiar ache in my heart for Aggie returned, and the laundry list of worries I had about for her future began to replay in my head.

I slowly closed the phone and looked at the giddy girl sitting next to me. "Oooh, Mommy I see more Christmas lights in Hobby Lobby! Are you ready? Let's go, let's go, let's go!" How does one jump from that phone call back into the joy of Christmas shopping? Once again I was startled by the dissonance I felt, the conflict between the joy of Christmas preparation and the pain that cast dark shadows over it all. It was a conflict that I carried the entire season long. Sometimes I did my best to fake it, other times I was too weary and tried my best to hide. Neither seemed to me to be healthy reactions. I did not know then that God slowly was teaching me something better than faking joy or hiding sadness.

Lorraine and I skipped into the store, and I did my best to push the ugly thoughts as far away as possible. It worked while we shopped, but as we drove home I began driving fast, anxious to hold and comfort my poor Aggie. While Lorraine relayed our shopping adventures to her daddy, I scooped Aggie into my arms and hugged her. As usual, she had no idea she needed comforting, but she was happy to allow Mommy to tuck her into bed for the night.

I lugged my sadness around with me the next day, and then to Advent service in the evening. I was not in the mood to be in public, or to celebrate much of anything, but I knew staying home and waiting for the next seizure was not likely to help anything either. The children and I filed into church together. Their eyes immediately were drawn to the tall, sparkling, cheerful Christmas tree in the front. Their giddy exclamations of "Mommy, look! Look at the angel! Look at the bows!" were met with tired responses, "Yes, I see, don't touch, sit down, not so loud." The cheer of the season just did not seem to be getting inside me this year. I longed for those Christmases of childhood, full of magic and family and Santa, uninterrupted by sadness and gloom. I guess I thought Christmas would always be that way, and

I was surprised and, in truth, rather offended, to find it so dreadfully difficult this year. The glitter and bells seemed out of place, even irritating to my aching heart.

Yet God's people sang on:

> *What child is this, who, laid to rest,*
> *On Mary's lap is sleeping?*
> *Whom angels greet with anthems sweet*
> *While shepherds watch are keeping?*
> *This, this is Christ the king,*
> *Whom shepherds guard and angels sing;*
> *Haste, haste to bring him laud,*
> *The babe, the son of Mary.*[3]

Though I did not really feel like "bringing him laud" at the moment, during the service I was taken up into the dramatic history of God's work. Though most of our nativity scenes nowadays are trimmed with lights and garland, the scene on that first Christmas day was not so rosy:

> *Why lies he in such mean estate*
> *Where ox and ass are feeding?*
> *Good Christian, fear; for sinners here*
> *The silent word is pleading.*
> *Nails, spear shall pierce him through,*
> *The cross be borne for me, for you;*
> *Hail, hail the word made flesh,*
> *The babe, the son of Mary.*[4]

The sadness and grief I felt so heavily were there too, in that scene with the sweet newborn babe, when God came to be with us. Violence, pain, and death were still to come for Him. He was born under that shadow just like us. The joy of His birth did not completely shatter the darkness, not right away, but even in that darkness there was a reason for rejoicing. As I sang and prayed with the church that evening, God gently took my eyes away from my own problems and reminded me simply of His great love for me, for Aggie, for everyone; love that we see most clearly in His Son Jesus.

Christians always have been people acquainted with grief, people whose hearts sometimes are torn with conflict; yet the church stubbornly and enthusiastically celebrates Christmas in the darkness of this world year after year. God gave us His very own Son, and because of Him we can see the nearness of God even in this place of pain. Our God does not stand far away, merely cheering us on through the darkness. He comes to dwell with us right in the middle of it.

It was Christmas time, and my family was surrounded with tangible reminders of the hope we have because *God is with us.* The lights of Christmas are not meant to point us merely to *this* world and *these* holiday pleasures; but to remind us that whether we rejoice here on earth or whether we grieve, "the darkness is passing away, and the true light is already shining" (1 John 2:8b). Candles flicker and we sing praises to the Light that has come into the world. Bells ring with joy as we remember promises made and fulfilled in Jesus. Glitter sparkles on angel wings and we look forward to the heavenly blessings to come when our Lord returns.

We dwell in darkness, but the love of Him who sent His Son shines brightly. And so, during our year of sadness, like every other year, God's children gathered together in the night, lifted up their heads, lit candles, and sang songs at the top of their voices, testifying to the world that God is indeed with us, and the darkness is passing away.

I was blessed to join God's children, to bring my aching heart to Him and to be filled with His love. My heart may have been weighed down by grief and worry, but because of Jesus I began to understand that we were suffering a mere trial, only temporary, and Christmas is about joy eternal. It is not flippant, unrealistic holiday joy that God gives. It is solid, based on the Word of God which cannot be moved. Today's pain will look so small when our joy in Christ finally is made complete.

Father, it is so easy to let the cares of this world overwhelm me. I have never faced something so awful as to watch my own child suffering like this, and forgive me, Lord, I do not know how to keep it from consuming me completely. Yet You are gracious, You know my pain and my weakness as well as hers. You have gently lifted up my head so that I once again see Your Son and remember Your great love for me and for Your daughter Aggie. Carry us through this trial, Lord, and hurry up and bring us home. Come, Emmanuel, come quickly.

Chapter 12
Silent Night

God was with us through the holidays, sometimes hauling us up off the ground after a bad day, other times encouraging us with small signs of hope. Very gradually, the medicine seemed to be helping Aggie's seizures. As I continued to add to my journal, I noticed an inconsistent but definite decrease in the number of seizures per day. I also noticed my dramatic descriptions of them were less frequent, which meant more and more of her seizures were short and relatively uneventful. During the mild seizures, she acted almost like someone simply hit her "pause" button for a few seconds, maybe a minute. When she was un-paused, she picked up right where she left off.

Several good days in a row filled me with all kinds of hope. I refused, at this point, to allow my picture of Aggie's future to contain seizures. It was only a few short months ago that she was fine. I was fairly confident that we just needed to find the right medicinal cocktail for her and she would be back to normal again. As winter came to our little town, it looked like her difficult days would be ending soon. Several weeks in a row passed with only two to three short seizures per day, and only an occasional long seizure that would disorient and exhaust her. It was still too much, but I saw it as major progress, and I was hopeful that the medicine would keep adjusting her back to health. During those days, for a change, epilepsy was not the first thing I thought of in the morning, nor what haunted me as I fell asleep at night.

As God carried me through those days, He gave me energy to make Christmas memories with the family and be in good spirits as much as possible. The beautiful services and songs of Advent helped me to adjust my focus, and, as I kept the next world in view, I thought about God's goodness and power, and I found my daily burdens a little easier to bear. I attempted to pass some of these sweet truths on to the children as well, with varying degrees of success.

Josh and I attempted to make Advent a time of devotion for the entire family. I taught the kids some new songs and their meanings during the day, and Josh led family devotions at night. It is not easy to create anything that resembles a devotional mood with children aged 5, 4, 2, and 1, but we tried. The kids taught us ways to make those events run a little more smoothly. For some reason, the candlelight from the Advent wreath cast a special mood over the whole experience for them, and caused them to lower their voices and become slightly more serious. To further keep the peace, I discovered I needed to make a chart so each child knew when it was his or her turn to pick a song or blow out the candles. We involved the kids in the telling of the Christmas story as much as possible, until, by the end of the month, the older children could tell most of it without assistance.

Through Josh's example, and fueled by the enthusiasm of the children, I became much more comfortable talking about God than ever before. It is not something that comes naturally to me, but experiencing His care for me through these difficult days gave me confidence. I was beginning to understand that His love is the only thing that keeps us steady as we travel through a world that is passing away. Slowly, I became more comfortable talking about these things with our children. Opportunities arose all the time, though I will not claim that they always went according to my plans.

For example, one ordinary day the children and I were waiting at a drive-through. After I ordered chicken nuggets and more chicken nuggets, I looked behind me and noticed that my sweet little Aggie in her pretty piggy tails had taken off her shoes and was licking them.

"Aggie! Don't lick your shoes!"

"Lick shoes?" asked Seth and commenced with his own meal of shoe germs in the backseat, and in kindness, also gave one of his shoes to little Marcus.

"KIDS!" I said. "Do you have any idea how many germs live on the bottoms of your shoes?"

Aggie suddenly became very serious. "Germs?"

"YES!" I said, sensing that this time she might actually listen to this lecture. "Your shoes pick up germs when you walk, and if you put them in your mouth they could make you very sick!"

"Oh…. Do my hands have germs now?" Her eyes were wide.

"Yes, in fact, let's wash them before we eat." I got out the hand sanitizer, wondering why the idea of germs seemed to be such a surprise when I know I had given this lecture at least a dozen times before.

Meanwhile, Aggie continued to worry aloud about germs in other places. "Are germs in my hair? The car? My shorts? The food? My carseat? My books? The dog?" With each affirmative answer from me, the panic in her voice increased a tiny bit more. Finally she sighed and asked, "Mommy, why did God make germs?"

That's a tough one, I thought. "Well, it's just part of living in a fallen world, Honey. There won't be any germs in heaven."

She suddenly sat up straight and smiled her huge Aggie smile, asking giddily, "So we can lick our shoes in heaven?!"

"Well…. I guess so…." Even if I had more to say on that subject, she wouldn't have heard a word. Her eyes were sparkling, and as she grinned and stared out the window, I could tell her mind was bursting with all the great things she will be able to lick in heaven when there are no germs to worry about.

Later that night I heard the girls bickering quietly in the back seat as we drove into town. All of a sudden Aggie said loudly, "YES, you can lick your shoes in heaven, Rainy, Mommy said so!"

"Aggie, you can NOT!" said Lorraine, obviously taken aback by the impropriety of the idea. Josh looked at me sideways, probably wondering what in the world I teach his children while he is away during the day. All I could do was laugh uncontrollably.

❦

The girls were learning "Joy to the World" and "Silent Night" with their Sunday school class for the Christmas Eve program. They knew the songs well, and sang them loudly, day after day after day, in preparation for the big night. One evening, I let them try on their beautiful Christmas dresses, and as soon as they were on, the girls thought it was time for a dress rehearsal. They took a standing coat rack from their room, removed their robes and hats, and before I could figure out what they were doing they explained, "Mommy, this is our microphone!" They hauled it out in front of the Christmas tree because the tree was beautiful like their dresses, and then they sang their little hearts out.

I got out the video camera. I put their performance on my blog for the grandparents who would not be able to make the program. They were like two cheerful little angels, grinning ear to ear while they shouted out the words to the songs. During "Silent Night" they got into a small argument about which part came next and what hand motions to do; but, other than that, they sang along in perfect little-kid harmony. I attempted to snatch up those good moments when they came, and in the instance of the dress rehearsal, I was very grateful that I did.

When Christmas Eve arrived, both girls were completely excited about the program. I enjoyed "making them beautiful" before we left for church that night. I put fancier-than-normal clothes on the boys too, but did not make much of a fuss about them because I did not want to incite rebellion. Seth, in particular, has very strong opinions about what he will or will not wear, and I have learned that anything that causes someone else to smile too big or gush too profusely is immediately suspect. He does not like to stand out. He had no intention of getting in front of a big crowd to sing Christmas songs that night.

As Josh and the boys and I sat in the pew and waited for the children to enter, I was holding my breath for Aggie. The congregation sang, and the children began to pour into church. The youngest kids went first, and I craned my neck to spot Aggie. Soon I realized that she was being carried, and I knew something was wrong. Her teacher brought her to me.

Apparently she had a seizure just before it was time to come in. Her enthusiasm was completely gone, and in its place was a tired stare. She was glad to see me and asked immediately, "When can we go home?" I took her in my arms and tried to get her to watch the other children perform. She was not interested. She sat on my lap, facing me, and snuggled me through the entire service, periodically asking, "When can we go home?" Lorraine grinned from ear to ear as she sang with all her might, while Aggie lay like a rag doll on my lap. I kept expecting Aggie's exhaustion to lift suddenly as it often did. When it was time for the littlest kids to go up and sing, I gave Aggie and Seth another shot. I went up front with them, but they would do nothing but crawl into my lap and bury their heads, Seth overcome by shyness, Aggie by fatigue. So I sat there like that with them during the two songs, while Lorraine and the others smiled and sang their hearts out. After the songs, I was relieved that somehow, I was able to get my pregnant self up from that position and safely back to the pew.

As I held tired Aggie through the rest of the service, it took all my energy to push back the grief and anger. *Epilepsy stole this moment from her.* I do not recall much of the Christmas program besides those awful feelings. Lorraine came home bursting with joy and asked, "Did you see me, Mommy? Wasn't that great?!" I did my best to match her enthusiasm. Aggie did not seem to realize that she had missed her chance to sing in front of everyone, and when she finally did pull out of her funk at home, she became her cheerful self again. I tried to block out the entire experience and held desperately to hope. *That was just a bump, just one little bad day.... she is getting better.*

Chapter 13
Queen Mommy

January brought a measure of calm to our house, as we recovered from the busyness of the holidays and enjoyed a long stretch of improved health. As the doctor continued to increase Aggie's medicine, she continued to have fewer seizures. Her seizures lasted mere seconds, and she almost never became disoriented or tired afterwards. Our safety concerns for her were not completely gone, but she was given a bit more freedom and we began to relax a little. For the moment, her epilepsy was not the enormous bug splatter in front of my nose that blocked my view of almost everything else. Although it was always somewhere in my peripheral vision, the problem had become much smaller.

Of course, children who have taken it upon themselves to stay on "seizure-alert" do not easily change those habits. Every day I would hear Seth or Lorraine yell, "Mommy! She's having a seizure!" and then right after that, "NO, I am NOT!" I would laugh and just carry on with my day. *She is definitely getting better.*

It was a crazy time in our lives even without seizures. Marcus suddenly learned to climb, and I often thought he seemed more like a mountain goat than a child. He always had at least two bruises somewhere on his face, but injuries never daunted him. At least ten times a day I would find myself saying in frustration, "Marcus! Where in the world did you get that?" He was an excellent stealer of toys and snacks, and the first child I have ever seen with the patience to plot and scheme and wait for just the right moment before he made his move. He showed signs of being an evil genius even at age one.

Seth, our oldest boy, constantly was irked by Marcus's trouble-making tendencies. He enjoyed having things in order, and even before he could walk he began cleaning up his toys without being asked! He probably wonders why in the world he was given a mommy like me. I am not terribly conscious of some of those things that are important to him. I fold laundry, but not always in perfect symmetry. I shove things in drawers and smash them closed. I let the crayons mix with the markers. I put away the toothpaste with the cap open. But Seth was patient with me, and continued his important job of closing cupboard doors and catsup lids for me whenever he could.

While Seth was showing me how to be more orderly, and Marcus and Aggie were trying to teach us all how to have more fun, Lorraine constantly was trying to make her world and everyone in it just a little more feminine. For me, this personality trait is the most foreign and strange of all. I always have been a tree-climbing, worm-catching kind of girl. Being dirty and disheveled is actually a virtue in my opinion, proof that one has had a good, productive day. When I was young, I much preferred riding bikes and playing soccer with the boys over Barbies and make-up. So how in the world did my firstborn turn out to be such a girly-girl? Lorraine didn't just "really, really, really" like the color pink. She liked, rather, she "love-love-loved!" any and everything flowery, lacy, pretty, glittery, or girly.

When I was growing up, I never really thought it was anything special to be a girl. It was something I accepted, and put up with, but never saw any reason to celebrate. In fact, things too girly have always been the objects of hearty, snorty laughter on my part. While I was pregnant with Lorraine some of that began to change. I was thrilled to be pregnant, feeling great, and enjoying every minute of it. I remember looking at maternity clothes with my mother one day, and I said "Oh, this is nice and feminine!" My old self screamed, *WHAT did you just say?* As my belly grew I was absolutely amazed at the wonder of it all. I even began wearing mascara, *every day*, and enjoying it!

Now my baby Lorraine is a big girl, and she has helped open my eyes to the joys of being a woman. It is not just having babies, it is nurturing, mothering, making the world around you welcoming and yes, even beautiful. I am only beginning to learn about these things, and I still have bouts of snorty laughter; but every now and then I try to play along with my princesses and act like a proper "Queen Mommy."

It was in the "Queen Mommy" spirit that I decided to make the girls princess canopies for their beds for Christmas this year. Of course, I needed someone much farther along in the arts of femininity to help me, so I asked Josh's mother. In reality, she allowed me to "help" her in the same way Marcus "helps" me clean the kitchen by licking the spoons. I learned a good deal watching her at work. She not only figured out an inexpensive way to make the canopies, but she also masterfully convinced her son that it was worth drilling a couple of holes in the ceiling for something so frivolous, I mean, decorative.

The girls absolutely loved their beds. When they saw them for the first time they squealed and begged to spend time alone in their "new" room for awhile. It did not take me long to realize that Aggie, like me, was still very much a princess-in-training. "No, Aggie, you can't swing from the canopy," I sighed, though I understood. While Aggie played just as hard as ever on her bed, Lorraine began to treat her entire room with a new-found respect. She would arrange her canopy and covers just so before she crawled into bed. Then she gently would lay back onto her pillow and draw the canopy around her. I am pretty sure that after I left the room, she would also sigh a dreamy sigh, fix her hair, and doze off thinking of princes and white horses.

I remember checking on the girls one night before I went to bed. I couldn't help but smile to myself when I saw Lorraine. She was sprawled out on her side, drooling on her pillow, her leg thrown over her covers, and her foot tangled in the canopy. I gently untangled her and covered her up again. She awoke, shocked to find herself in such a state. She looked at me wide-eyed and said, "Oh, thank you, Mommy," as she quickly arranged herself like a proper princess again.

Giggle, snort.

Chapter 14
Belly Growth and Grace

I am so glad that unborn children are relatively low-maintenance. Granted, I can only say that because I have incredibly easy pregnancies, but especially during this year of moving and changes and epilepsy, I was grateful that at least *one* of my children required very little of me. I was nearing my third trimester, and my newest baby boy asked only to be hauled around wherever I happened to go, which, at this stage, did not even require the use of my arms. It is true what they say about large families: it is impossible to give successive children the attention you gave your firstborn. When I was pregnant with Lorraine, I kept a pregnancy journal which ended up being over twenty single-spaced pages long. I did start a journal that year for Eldon, but only found time to write in it twice. Those two entries fill a mere one page.

It does not seem to matter how many times I have been pregnant before; I am always completely amazed at the entire process. It is such an enormous miracle, going on right inside my own body. Even during busy days or seizure-filled days, days when I was overwhelmed with everything else and temporarily forgot I was growing another child, God's work continued, and my son grew just as he should. I feel like I had almost no part in it at all. Growing a brand new human person is so complex and intricate, and so obviously a job way above my own skill level. God does amazing work, in me and through me, and lets me be a part of it and share in the joy and wonder.

But, by the third trimester, both the baby and my belly were getting so big that I rarely forgot I was pregnant any more. I was much thinner in my mind than I was in reality, which explains why I often bumped into things. I am not typically what you would call graceful, but at the end of my pregnancies, the clumsiness becomes ridiculous. Even my little Aggie, who was usually too busy having fun to make observations of any kind, said to me one day, "Mommy, you look like you have a penguin butt!"

Many times I noticed this handicap during those sweet moments when I snuggled a child to sleep. When the child finally started snoring away, I knew it was time to sneak out. I would lay there a few moments longer, mentally going over my body trying to guess which muscles would actually work when I called on them. I would come up with an elaborate strategy and finally get up the nerve to give it a try. Muscles would contract and pull, arms and legs flail, I would stifle a yelp, and end up on the floor. After a deep breath, I would check on the child who, usually, was still sleeping. I then gingerly would crawl out of the room and thank God that my husband was not watching.

As my belly grew, I tried to think of creative ways to delegate some of the housework. We have a huge, wide-open basement that has become the kids toy wonderland. They have a craft center, a small television, plenty of toys, and even enough space to ride small bikes. As I began nesting, I noticed that the much-used wrestling mats needed a good cleaning. Yet for me, cleaning any part of the house below my knees, was extremely uncomfortable. *Hmmmm...I* thought. *I have a few little people who live much closer to these dirty floors than I do, and they do not have to choke on baby feet or last night's dinner every time they bend over...how could I get them to help me?*

One day, when school was cancelled due to snow, I had a brilliant idea. I called it "summer play time." I told my kids, who were bursting with cabin fever, that we were going to pretend it was summer in our basement. They could not believe I was letting them put on their swimsuits and wear them to the "lake" in the basement (the blue gym mats). Of course, the lake needed water (warm soapy water) which they cheerfully scrubbed all over the mats. Then they pretended it was a Slip-N-Slide. When they got tired of that I got out a scrub brush (which they fought over!) and let them play "car wash" while they washed down their bikes and cars and other toys. Even Seth got into that game, and soon my basement floors, the mats, and all the toddler toys were shiny and clean! While all this cleaning was going on, my big belly and I sat on the couch laughing and taking pictures.

The kids were generally compassionate towards my awkwardness, and tried to accept my excuses for sitting out of wrestling matches and taking a break from dance parties. I think I may have increased my complaints at this stage, because once or twice I heard Lorraine say, "Oh, my back really aches tonight." Aggie prayed for me once during family devotions, in her wild Aggie way all in one breath, "Please watch over the shepherds taking care of their sheep so the sheep don't run away and bless Mommy so she doesn't puke up tonight and thank you for chocolate milk and Peter Pan Amen."

Pregnancy hormones were not something I could explain to the kids, however, or even to my husband or myself. God kept our family together through my aches and pains and changing moods and fatigue, and my instability often made me newly grateful for His grace. I saw how He cared for my family on days when I could not, and I felt His care for me through my husband and friends who encouraged me when I needed it. In the sunshine of those days, it was fairly easy to smile and be glad that God loves me, that He is full of mercy and grace towards me. And it was a mercy, while I was feeling overwhelmed with those minor troubles, that He did not let me see how much more I would need His grace to face the trials that would come next.

Chapter 15
February Chill

One of the scariest things about epilepsy is that nobody, not even doctors, seem to know for certain where it is headed. Through the holidays and most of January, Aggie seemed to be on a steady path towards getting better. Seizures no longer were terrifying for us, and we all began to feel that if she did not soon return to full health, which we expected, at least she would maintain some sort of predictable, manageable state. We did not know then that a long stretch of good days could be just as deceiving as cancer in remission. Just when it seems that the enemy is defeated and health is right around the corner, it can come back with a shocking violence and shatter the world once more.

I allowed myself to become comfortable with her again, and began to pretend I had things pretty much under control, at least as much as I could pretend such a thing with four loose children and one jumping around in my womb. Yet my heart was as fragile and changeable as Aggie's health.

I remember one morning, during the comfortable chaos of getting Lorraine ready for school, changing diapers, tying shoes, and taking sips of my cold coffee whenever I remembered I still had it, when I first noticed that Aggie's seizures were starting to change again. She was jabbering away and walking down the long hallway towards me when her eyes looked up and she began to go into a seizure. A common sight, but I set the laundry down and intended to stay close to her for the ten seconds I expected it to last. She continued to look up, but I noticed her entire face looked like it was taken over by the seizure: no muscle tone at all, and a completely blank expression. As I watched, the weakness seemed to spread to her shoulders and down her body, and she tipped towards the wall. I immediately grabbed her and held her so she would not fall. Before I had a chance to see what the seizure would do next, she lifted up her head and began talking. Typically, this would mean she was "back" and the seizure was over. As I took a breath in relief, I noticed that she was muttering, not making sense, and looking off into the distance while she spoke. "Aggie? Aggie, what are you talking about?" I asked as I tried to make sense of her behavior. Then, just as quickly as it started, the muttering stopped, and she ran off down the hallway.

I followed her to the living room, where I found her on the couch, curled up under a blanket. "Mommy, can I watch some TV? I want to watch Curious George." she said. She was obviously back in her right mind, though tired. I turned on the television for her and snuggled her. I could only sit for a moment, as the tasks of the day continued their relentless calling to me. I got up and went through the motions of filling sippy cups, brushing teeth, and sending Lorraine off to school.

I tried to keep my thoughts under control as I did the jobs of the day, though my heart was racing. *That was just a bump. She is getting better.* I kept Aggie a little closer to me, and obsessively watched her every move. She spent an hour on the couch, and showed no interest in the boys' wrestling match which took place right under her feet that morning. *She doesn't even notice their giggles? Unprecedented.* Yet after her rest she seemed her cheerful, talkative self. *See, she's fine again. But…do her eyes look sunken again, or is it just me?* No matter; whether her eyes were sick-looking or not, the laundry needed to be done and the kids needed something to do, so we did our best to go on with our day. Though I grumbled about it then, I now see the blessing God gave me in the work that was in front of me all day, every day. I am certain my emotions and worries would have consumed me were it not for the sheer amount of little things that constantly required my attention.

That one incident filled me with new anxiety, which again fueled my observations, writing, and research. I cannot pretend this was even helpful in the long run, but it was one small way I made myself feel like I was doing something, anything, to help Aggie. As I watched her that day, I saw a few short, "normal" seizures, and a few more "weird" ones. I waited anxiously for a chance to talk to Josh about these new observations.

Josh is a stable, objective, and scientific person, and he provided a good balance to my perspective, which was influenced by mommy-love and panic. When I gave him the day's Aggie report, he immediately filled me in on the technical side of things: the movement and the muttering are called "automatisms," and indicate that the seizures are spreading to a different part of the brain.

But what does that mean? Is this a bad sign or a good one? Does it mean we are on the wrong track with the medicine? What do we do about it? And worst of all, does this mean her seizures are going to just keep getting worse and worse?

The only things we knew for sure was that it was something new. It was something that created new safety concerns and made more of a scene in public. It was something unsettling to watch, something I would have to see and prepare for and potentially protect her from each day. I called her doctor, who made a note, and ordered yet another increase of her medicine, and decided it was time to schedule another test, this time a 24-hour EEG. Again, we watched and waited and had no idea what was to come.

◦✖◦

By the day of her next EEG, the seizures seemed to be calming down again, and we even discussed the possibility of not putting her through test at all. She had five seizures the day before the test, but each one was short and mild, and again we were confident that medicine would to fix her problems any day now. Besides that, neither of us wanted to spend 24 hours in a hospital room with a wiggly little girl who must stay in bed, especially if it might not be necessary! However, the waiting lists tended to be pretty long for this kind of test, so we decided we might as well get it done while she had a spot.

Aggie and Daddy got up by 6 a.m. to get ready for the test that day. The other children heard them, and soon everyone was awake wondering what was going on. We explained that Aggie had to go to the hospital for another test, and this time she and Daddy had to stay all night long. We huddled together on couches to pray as a family before they left. In that moment, Josh and I were the strong, calm parents, encouraging nervous children to find peace in God's love. *Jesus, go with Aggie and Daddy and watch over them during her test, and please care for Mommy and the other children at home. Amen.*

I was surprised to find some relief that day as I stayed home with the other children. Friends from church made certain we were well cared for, somehow knowing that both food and company would keep me sane and help pass the long hours. Though my heart was still with Aggie, I tried to take advantage of the rare opportunity I had to put the seizure antenna away and truly focus on the healthy children.

I knew Josh had a much more challenging day ahead of him, as he attempted to entertain Little Miss Party Starter in a hospital bed all day long. While she enjoyed books, movies, and computer games, it was not possible to keep her satisfied with these things for an entire day. As we should have expected, she found her own small ways to make her stay more exciting. They were in a very small room with no bathroom, so they gave her a little commode. Every time she used it, Daddy had to take it to the bathroom to empty it out. She thought this was absolutely *hilarious,* so she went to the bathroom as often as she could! I can just picture her eyes sparkling as she said, "Daddy, I have to go potty again!"

Though she had had five seizures the day before, she only happened to have one during those entire 24 hours in the hospital, and it was a short one. While this was rather discouraging to us, we were assured the doctors could tell quite a bit just from her regular brain activity.

When they returned home the next day, Josh was exhausted; but Aggie was her wild, cheerful self. She was so happy to be free of the wires and out of that tiny room that she spent the day wrestling and playing hard with her sister and brothers. *It's nice to have her back,* I thought. The EEG confirmed her brain was prone to seizures, and the doctor recommended we stay the course and give her current medicine more time to work. Because I could not see what was to come, I continued to hold on to the hope that any minute now, we would have a *healthy* Aggie back, too.

Chapter 16
A Short List

Because I am a list-maker by nature, very few days begin slowly and continue aimlessly when I am in charge. At the very least, I have a mental list of to-dos, goals and objectives. As soon as Lorraine could draw, I realized she was much like me: fond of making lists, and even more fond of checking things off her list. I involved her in the plan for that day, and her input and enthusiasm as we wrote a list together truly helped the day go more smoothly. List-making became a common ritual for the children and me from that day on. Often we would create our list while we ate breakfast, and each child would suggest something he would like to do that day. If it was reasonable, I put it on the list. The children felt that they had a little control over the day. If I knew I had to make phone calls or do major housework, I would schedule activities for the children that required less of my attention, followed by others that allowed me to be more engaged. Sometimes I let each child schedule fifteen minutes of "Mommy time," when they got to have Mommy all to themselves and choose the activity. We also began using a timer, as I discovered one of the keys to keeping the children cheerful is changing up the activity just before they get bored—about every 20-30 minutes for my children.

My husband simply does not understand my task-oriented nature. In fact, when he saw Lorraine making lists and checking things off, he approached me in all seriousness and asked, "Do you really think you should be encouraging that?" Granted, we who are task-oriented may have difficulty "relaxing" or watching an entire movie, and we may attempt to wash your dishes before you are done with them, but we accomplish more before 9 a.m. than most people do in an entire day! I am sure that if my husband really understood how much he personally benefits from those of us who are task-oriented, he would tease us a little less. I might even quit doing my daily tasks and see how he fairs without his clean shirts and hot meals.... I might, if that were possible for someone like me. However, those things are on the list. They must be done.

I tried to keep our lives going as usual even during Aggie's difficult days, but her new seizures presented new challenges. During the weeks that followed, she continued to add strange behaviors to some of her seizures, and these longer seizures also seemed harder on her physically. One minute we might be having a rowdy good time at the park, then one of these seizures would strike, and suddenly Aggie required an hour-long nap. We would have other days full of mere short seizures, when Aggie would act like her high-energy, cheerful self all day long. Neither her energy level nor her mood nor anything else gave us any kind of hint as to which kind of day it would be.

I kept on forming my little mental plans for the day, but more often than not Aggie's problems would blow my list to bits. When I could, I kept all possible plans from the children, as I knew they could be changed at any moment. "I'm sorry, Honey, we just have to wait and see how Aggie is doing." I said that often, much too often, to the other children. They wanted to make the lists. They wanted to go to the library. They wanted me to promise they would receive fifteen minutes of undivided attention that day. I tried, but my seizure antenna was always on high alert, and Aggie's needs trumped everything else.

My control over our lives and our days was slipping away, as was my hope for her imminent return to health. Relentlessly the seizures came and came, increasing in intensity and always changing. Each new development was a new wound, and a new worry.

One day, as I was working in the kitchen, the kids were playing everywhere throughout the house. My seizure antenna was on as always, though my eyes were on the dishes and my mind on that night's dinner. Suddenly I sensed a problem, a silence that was out of place, or some sort of danger. "Aggie?" I called down the hallway. No answer. I quickly looked in each room and did not see her. *She must be downstairs.* I opened the door to the basement stairs. It was unusually heavy. As I pulled the door open, I pulled Aggie with it. She had been teetering on the top step, her arm stretched out behind her, gripping the handle to the basement door. She was deep within a seizure. I pulled her away from the stairs and held her on my lap as the seizure continued. Eventually it washed over her, she came "back," and ran off to find the other children. *How long had she been like that? What if she had let go?* My anxious thoughts circled around all evening, as I went through the motions of serving dinner, reading bedtime stories, and tucking children into bed.

More frequent, dangerous seizures, and more dramatic recovery times meant that Aggie was requiring more and more care. Her needs began to dictate how we spent each day, each hour. I did my best to keep things as normal as possible for the other children, still trying to make time for play-dough and wrestling and reading books. Often these things were interrupted, but sometimes they were not. Yet even when Aggie did not require something of me, my heart was always divided. When I wasn't directly tending to her needs, I was trying to cope with my own feelings, trying to push back the waves of grief that threatened to consume me on the bad days. I had crossed almost everything off of my list, and replaced my goals with one essential thing: TO SURVIVE.

Chapter 17
To Aggie, My Nap Buddy

Aggie Sue, I love when you are my nap buddy. To see my little tornado still and calm is a rare treat. I love the way you ask to hold my hand until you fall asleep.

Today you had a long seizure right before nap time that made you so tired you were asleep in my bed even before I laid down the other kids. I climbed in next to you anyway. I just wanted to be close to you. I held your little hand.

Like so many times before, I rested next to you and stroked your hair. My heart loved and ached, and my eyes were relieved to release a few tears that had been sitting there all day. As I sighed over your raccoon eyes and stroked your hair, I wondered where on that beautiful head they would cut should they have to do surgery. My spirit prayed fervently to the God who loves us both.

We laid there in the sunshine, and you snored peacefully as I wrestled with my worries. The sun shone brightly even through the blinds, and soon I found myself relaxing into the quiet and warmth of the bed.

I thank God for that moment, when you and I lay there in the sun, wrapped in warm blankets and love, enjoying a green pasture before our journey through the valley.

We have darkness to go through yet, my dear child. I am sure we often will hold hands through the darkness as we are doing now. I suspect we will be separated for some of it. I know we will be carried through all of it by Him who loves us both, the One who has been there before. But for this sweet moment, we rest on our pillows that smell like home.

I wonder, after the days of valleys and darkness, will we be given moments like this again? Will we rest together, hold hands, and enjoy the warmth of each others' love on pillows that smell like Home? Will we give goodnight kisses, smile, say I love you for the millionth time, in that Other place?

Perhaps then the shadows of this valley will be distant memories. Perhaps the sun will be the Light of Christ, the light that chased away our fears and pain, and our "I love yous" will finally be sweet and pure and simple.

Chapter 18
Darkness Descends

The life and sunshine of springtime were for other people that year. Inside our home, we were surrounded by an ever-increasing darkness. Aggie's condition grew steadily worse, and the sickness that was taking her away was consuming all of us.

Anyone and everyone who was close to our family during this time suffered right along with us. Tons of people were concerned and praying, constantly calling and emailing to inquire, "How's Aggie?" I wrestled with my own emotions whenever I was asked this question. Do I tell our family from out-of-state how bad Aggie was today, knowing it will only make them sad and they can do nothing to help? In vain, I tried to shield others from suffering along with us.

But they did suffer; those who let our little hummingbird into their hearts also had their hearts broken as they saw how she was slipping away during these months. Because it was easier than talking about these things in person, I sometimes shared my feelings with loved ones on my blog:

March 2009
I know some people have been keeping up with this blog, but you just don't know what to say anymore. I just want you to know I know that, and it is ok. I don't know what to say either. I don't like to be the person whose very presence reminds everyone of this huge sad thing, nor do I like Aggie to be that person. But we do, and we all feel a bit uncomfortable about that. We are in a time of trial, but

even though it hurts, we all know God is doing something here...we just don't know what it is.

Family, friends, and church family surrounded us in those days. When words seemed futile, people gave us meals and babysitting and listening ears. As we suffered together, we also reassured each other that our God *is* a loving God, and He cares for us even when we do not understand what He is doing. And we certainly did not understand what He was doing.

�֍

As I watched Aggie have seizures every day, I gradually learned how to care for her in different situations. Every situation became much more complicated and stressful when I factored in potential seizures. Childhood hazards are challenging enough for mothers whose kids do not have seizures. Aside from Aggie, I had Lorraine learning how to use the monkey bars, Seth right on her heels, and Marcus, not yet two, who thought he could do absolutely everything the older children could do. I also had a body stretched and off-balance, bursting with child number five. My reactions were not so quick, my aerobics less than graceful.

With healthy children, parents teach them while looking forward to the day when they can reasonably trust them. Though Marcus was young, he was quite coordinated, and I knew he would have no trouble with the stairs to the big slide, for example. I knew it would only take a few times working with him to teach him how to balance on a swing. Children gradually grow more independent, and more capable. They do not want to get hurt, and they learn ways to keep themselves safe.

When I had Aggie at the park, I could see the extreme problem that seizures posed for her. When a child has seizures, they never, ever will be trustworthy or safe on a climbing wall, a swing, or a slide. Seizures strike without warning, and the child has absolutely no control over his body for as long as the seizure lasts. There is no time to get down from the monkey bars. There is no time to call for help. Seizures came, ravaged Aggie's little body, and cared nothing about the consequences.

I was often angry about this extra problem of seizures. It was such an interruption to our "normal" lives and Aggie's "normal" childhood. Right or wrong, that anger made me more determined to allow Aggie to do as many "normal" things as possible. I realized that her new problems created new jobs for me, and if I wanted her to experience some of the usual joys of childhood, I would have to assume the extra stress and responsibility on her behalf. The wide open spaces of the playground no longer provided a moment's peace for me. If we went somewhere, I literally laced up my running shoes, and determined to stay on my toes for Aggie. I hovered, I kept my antenna on high alert, and I did what I could to keep her safe.

I cannot overstate the constant guilt I felt towards the other children. Not only were they getting less and less of Mommy every day; but even when they did have Mommy, she was very rarely "fun Mommy" any more. They felt the worry and tension in our home, and they bore Aggie's burdens in their own way. They suffered various small injustices, missed a few social events, and lived for months in "survival mode" as we managed Aggie's seizures.

That spring, Aggie began to experience more of what we called "melting" seizures. This kind of seizure came on gradually, always with her looking up and to the right, and slowly took away the muscle tone from her entire body.

If nobody was there to catch her, she would slump down slowly to the floor. Occasionally, she would also have slight tremors in her head and hands during this kind of seizure.

I will never forget how Lorraine learned to watch for the signs and help in any way she could. She was only six years old then, yet countless times she saved her sister from injury just by being aware. I remember going downstairs to check on the kids, and finding Aggie with her back arched, completely limp in Lorraine's arms. They had been riding bikes when the seizure came, and Lorraine instinctively protected Aggie from cracking her head on the concrete floor. I remember times playing outside, and times when the girls were alone in their room, when Lorraine either caught Aggie herself or quickly alerted me so that I could protect her. I remember sending Lorraine for supplies while I held a bleeding Aggie and waited for a seizure to finish. Lorraine, already instinctively nurturing and protective, was bearing all kinds of adult responsibilities as she learned how to assist in emergencies. Though I would rather have protected her from all of these experiences, I saw God giving her the strength to bear it. Her heart was facing troubles beyond her age, but God greatly fortified her in faith, and she never doubted His love.

One beautiful spring evening the girls and I took a walk down our country road. We talked excitedly of the new baby that was to come—in a couple weeks or so, I told them. Lorraine, ever fascinated with babies, asked me "Mommy, why do the doctors not know what day that baby will come? Why do they just have to guess?"

"Well, Honey, there are still lots of things even doctors don't know about our bodies or how God made us. We still get sick...there are still some things doctors don't know how to fix."

"Mommy!" she said excitedly, as though stumbling upon a terrific original thought, "If God were here, nobody would ever get sick again!"

I opened my mouth to take advantage of the opportunity to say something about God's care for us during sickness, about the cross, or the about the good things that can come from suffering, but as I took a breath, the grief that I had been carrying all day about Aggie came rushing up my throat. Images filled my head: *Six seizures so far today. That one on top of the slide could have been disastrous had I not caught her. Her weepy eyes, her confusion—are they from the newest medicine that is only making things worse?* It took all my energy to get my breath back. I turned my eyes to the woods and used all of my strength to hold back my tears. In true kid fashion, Lorraine quickly forgot what we were talking about and moved on to something else.

When night came, the children slept peacefully as always. I lay in bed awake, her comment still haunting me.

Marcus has a high fever and an awful cough tonight.

If God were here.....

I just woke Aggie to make sure she was okay. I could hardly wake her...is it because it is midnight, because she just had another seizure, or because the anti-seizure medicine is hurting her sweet body already?

If God were here...

I listened to my husband breathing and wrestled with my thoughts. The child in my womb kicked and squirmed, bursting with life even before he saw his first glimpse of the world. I thought of Lorraine, Seth, and Marcus; of their different personalities and gifts; and of their health and vigor. And I thought of Aggie, whose cheerfulness and vitality seemed to be draining away before my eyes.

Tears flowed silently out of my eyes as I tried to pray. My mind was cluttered and my emotions were so loud, I could form no words. I simply lay before the Lord and showed Him my pain.

Oh, God, why do you make some flowers bloom and let others wither?

Chapter 19
Empty Mommy

Nights that began in grief and worry did not often end in restful sleep. Pregnancy aches woke me often, and every return to consciousness also brought a flood of unpleasant thoughts and fears. Fitful nights turned into busy mornings long before I was rested. As soon as I got out of bed I was met with a list of demands and constant kid chatter. I needed more than coffee to cope with those days.

Some of those days were successfully completed, albeit in survival mode, and I went to bed feeling that I had done the best I could under the circumstances. But there were also very bad days, days when the grief would almost consume me. I would walk around feeling utterly empty, like a cup with an enormous hole in the bottom. All energy, patience, joy, enthusiasm for life, love, strength, and everything good about me just drained out of the hole. Anything in the world that ever brought me joy only brought irritation and annoyance. Any kind of experience at all, even a playful kiss from one of my children, felt like something that sucked energy, life, patience out of me. All I could see in the world was need after need after need that I simply could not meet.

My body screamed with exhaustion, so that even one mere dish in the sink seemed like an overwhelming task and personal insult. I became exceedingly selfish in every single one of my thoughts: my mental ranting was constant and loud, and consisted only of complaints and guilt. I saw my family and saw nothing but my guilt and failures. My heart simply could not give them the love they deserved. If there was a conflict between the children or a discipline issue to be addressed, my emotional state was such that I only had two options: seethe in silence or overreact. I did not trust myself to be a fair judge for the children, so I withdrew as much as possible. I remember praying, *God help me be kind to the children for just five lousy minutes. Help me get them to bed without those feelings of frustration, without a nasty tone of voice or dirty look.*

My thoughts were filled with self-pity mixed with a thousand "shoulds," and prayers for help and forgiveness that felt unanswered. *You should not feel this way, you should be thankful for your children, for your home, for your husband and your health. You should be kind and patient, you should be thinking of others, you should be able to make it through a meal without slamming your hand on the table and yelling! You should not use words that wound your children, you should not think your life is so hard, you should not have this terrible attitude toward those you say you love. You should be able to pull yourself together and function!*

Lord, forgive me, help me, change my heart. Lord, forgive me, forgive me, forgive me. Help me, O God, please, help me. I am a mess. Jesus, help.....

I remember many mornings, hiding in the office with my coffee while the children watched cartoons, in tears even before breakfast. I have heard many people say that "God never gives you any more than you can handle." I am sure there are good intentions behind those words, but that thought did not seem to match the reality I was facing. There was no secret strength inside my heart that I was now discovering. I was not demonstrating how strong I really could be. I was *far* beyond what I could handle on my own at this point. I was curled up in a ball, crying on the deck of the ship while the storm raged on.

When I came before the Lord, I had trouble assembling any thoughts to form a prayer. I was simply an enormous pit of need. I was weak, selfish, and completely empty-handed. My cup was empty, and everything I tried to put in it to fill myself up again just fell out the hole in the bottom.

God, I have nothing. I prayed, as I sat with my empty hands open on my desk. *I have nothing but there are needs everywhere around me. My children need their mother. They need breakfast, they need playfulness and love. Yet I only have self-pity and depression. Have mercy on me, Lord.*

As I sat there in tears, my Aunt's words came back to me again: *weak and loved.* Again and again I needed to re-learn this lesson. Why am I always surprised at my own weakness? God is not. He loves the weak, He fills my empty hands. I cannot count how many times He pulled me out of the pit of depression and set me back on my feet.

The trial was about Aggie, of course; yet, for me, it was about me and my own difficulties. Those days of exhaustion truly made me see the selfishness of my heart and my own helplessness to overcome sin. I wanted her better for my sake. I wanted to close my heart to her so that I did not have to hurt every time I looked at her. I wanted to know why. I wanted an easy answer, health for everyone, and uneventful, pleasant days. At the very least, I wanted to be able to care for her without having to suffer myself.

God said no to each and every one of these wants. His plans for me and for my family were nothing like my own. Yet He wanted to pour out His mercy on me. He wanted me to learn that more than any other blessing in this world, there is nothing so wonderful as His grace. As He always does during the season of Lent, He pointed me again to the cross of Christ. The suffering and pain that had come into my life that year exposed my pathetic version of love, and revealed the ugly, awful selfishness in my own heart. I saw suffering and pain overwhelm Jesus on the cross, too. Yet in that instance, suffering only made His love shine brighter. I saw Him, Jesus, who loves me, taking on my ugliness and bearing it for me.

He saw my empty hands and my guilt, but God showed me in Jesus how much He loves me. His love for me was constant and strong, even on the days when I was nothing but an empty cup with a hole in the bottom. I was weak, but I was loved. He wanted me to trust Him, and to love those around me, including sick Aggie, even though it would hurt. Yet He never expected me to do that on my own. He gently said no to many of my wants and demands, but He gave me gifts I did not know enough to ask for. Some days it seemed that He fixed my cup, and even filled it with His blessings. Other days depression would nearly overcome me; but I learned that though my emotions were unpredictable and fickle, His love would never let me go.

If God were *not* here, I would have remained curled up in the fetal position, crying into my coffee. He pulled me up and made me function again. As I look back on this trial, I can see His hand much more clearly. I see those good things I seemed to have—the strength, the love and endurance—and I know they were not something I dragged out of the deep recesses of my inner being. They were gifts, purely gracious gifts from my loving Father.

Loving sick Aggie hurt terribly, every single day. God did not answer my burning questions, but He did care for me and for her. He opened my eyes and taught me where to look for His gifts. He did not so animate this weak body so that I conquered this trial like a warrior; but He carried me, strengthened my heart and my faith, and made me function. It may not have been what I was looking for, but it was certainly a miracle.

As the deer pants for flowing streams,
so pants my soul for you, O God.
My soul thirsts for God, for the living God.
When shall I come and appear before God?
My tears have been my food day and night,
While they say to me all the day long,
"Where is your God?"
These things I remember as I pour out my soul:
how I would go with the throng and lead them
in procession to the house of God
with glad shouts and songs of praise,
a multitude keeping festival.
Why are you cast down, O my soul?
and why are you in turmoil within me?
Hope in God; for I shall again praise him,
my salvation and my God.
(Psalm 42:1-6a)

Chapter 20
Aggie Who?

Individual seizures are said to have no harm on a person's brain. However, there seems to be some kind of cumulative effect on those who have frequent seizures. Not only that, but every one of the many drugs we gave Aggie had potential cognitive side effects. And of course, there was that abnormality in her brain. The cause we did not know, but we were definitely beginning to see major personality changes in our little girl.

Basic skills of daily living, those little things a typical four year old can do for herself, I truly took for granted when Aggie was healthy. "Aggie, go get dressed for the day, Honey." It was a simple request, one she had been able to fulfill cheerfully and quickly for more than a year. As her sickness began to change her, simple commands became quite a challenge for Aggie. I remember her attempting to get herself dressed, but being overtaken by a seizure in her room. I walked by and discovered her muttering to herself and walking in circles, over and over and over. Another time she left intending to obey, but she noticed crayons on her floor that needed to be put back in the crayon box. She put them back one at a time. Then she dumped them out on the floor, and patiently put them back again one by one. She repeated this behavior for over thirty minutes when I finally intervened.

Though she had always been a dramatic child, during these days she seemed to experience nothing but extremes. She was either wildly energetic and happy, or nearly passed out on the couch. She might be able to hyper-focus on a story or a craft, or she could be entirely too distracted to speak in a complete sentence. She might be a party-starting social butterfly, or want nothing other than to sit alone in her room and do something quiet (and often repetitive). Some days she was incredibly oral: licking, chewing, and biting on strange things. Other days she was what I can only describe as "slippery." Her mind was in such a state that I had a hard time getting her attention so I could communicate with her. Several times a day I would say things like "Aggie, Aggie, Aggie, Aggie, AGGIE, put on your shoes, Honey! Aggie, put on your shoes, Aggie, Aggie, Aggie, here are your shoes! Put them on!"

She took the concept of "living in the present moment" to a new level. Many days it seemed like she was literally incapable of thinking of anything other than what was in her direct line of vision. Sometimes this was a good thing, as when I told her it was time to go to the doctor and get her blood drawn. She cheerfully colored all the way there, chatted about whatever she saw in front of her, and did what she was told. When the needle was in she screamed hear heart out, but the second it was over it seemed like the whole experience had fallen completely out of her brain and she again was enjoying her coloring book. Other times this was a real problem. She may have intended to call her sister and brothers for supper, but noticed her favorite book lying in the closet, where she would sit and read it repeatedly until someone found her.

The difficulties each little behavior presented were minor in themselves, but the challenge was in knowing how to manage them, or help her manage them. I was never quite sure whether I was seeing some uncontrollable effect of her sickness or her medicine, or simply a four year old testing her boundaries in need of a little direction. Do I nag her for chewing on her hair, or is she simply expressing anxiety in the only way she knows how? Is it even reasonable to try to get her to sit still during church, or has it become impossible? Why in the world can she follow three-part directions today when yesterday she could not even remember one simple request?

There was no easy way to sort out these things, so Josh and I did the best we could; sometimes simply taking a wild guess. Her doctor seemed to think most of the things I was describing sounded like normal four-year-old behavior. But I had a strong memory of the "old" Aggie, and I was certain that most of these new quirks were definitely *not her*. The wild guessing, the guessing wrong, and the pure hard work of it all often frustrated me to the point of tears.

Jesus, she was so pathetic this morning after that long seizure! It took her an hour to recover! How is she going to be helped? Is she at all? I am so concerned for her safety. I am constantly wondering whether I am making the right call to let her or not let her (and all the others) do certain things. My anxiety is even spilling over into my dreams! Jesus, your grace is so very important.... how would I make it through, in view of my failings, if I did not know of your unconditional love? You have taken hold of me and are dragging me towards life and salvation though I fight and whine all the while. Help it not to get too dark, Lord. Sustain me through what is coming. Most of all, keep the darkness out of my heart. Please fight off fear, despair, and depression for me, Jesus. I am so tired.

Oh, Jesus, hold me close.

After trying another medicine and yet another increase of the first one, it seemed nothing would even begin to slow the frequent, intense seizures. Seven to ten times per day she would be overcome by a seizure, and that is only counting the roughly 11 hours per day when she was awake. Her doctor scheduled another MRI at the end of March. We took her again, she hated it again, and then we held our breaths as we waited for test results.

Awaiting yet another round of potentially life-changing test results, I went from calm to frazzled and back again ten times before 8 a.m. on the day of the impending phone call. *Lord, it is so easy for me to get overwhelmed and unreasonably irritated at the little things, like toys on the floor. Is this my way of trying to control SOMETHING while other things must spin out of control? If it is, it doesn't work and I need to quit it! It drives me and everyone else nuts! A perfectly shiny floor will not help Aggie's epilepsy go away.*

My clean house gave me no answers, but neither did the MRI. The spot had not changed, and no other problems appeared. So we continued on the same course, trying and waiting for different medicines to help. It was hard to believe that this was the best that modern medicine could do for my sick child, and it was hard to stand by as she continued to get worse and worse. While we followed the doctor's orders, we continued to investigate anything else in the world that might help our sick little girl.

Josh's parents wanted to take the three older children to Hilton Head for spring break that year. We initially said they could, with the understanding that Aggie's condition might change things for her. As the time got closer, she got sicker, and I struggled greatly trying to decide what to do about spring break. It was extremely difficult for me to trust anyone else, even grandparents, to care for Aggie. Yet how could we let the others go and make her stay home? She was having major problems, but she was functioning and still capable of having fun. Her health was definitely not perfect, but we were beginning to think it never would be. None of us said it out loud, but the obvious stared us in the face. *This may be her last chance to have a vacation. She may not get better. She may not even be here next year.*

Trusting someone else with my children is like trusting them with my very heart. It is never easy. This time it took an extra amount of prayer and effort for me to let them go. I remember thinking up little reasons why maybe they should stay home, calling my husband, and then realizing even as I was speaking and before he began to "talk me down" that I was simply venting anxiety. It was good practice for me to let them go, to allow even Aggie out of my sight and out of my hands for several days. *My children are not my own,* I told myself repeatedly and forcefully, *and they are safe in God's hands even when they are not in mine.*

Chapter 21
An Interruption of Life

God must have known how badly I needed a break at that time. I was right at the end of my pregnancy and completely exhausted, harassed by aches and pains and insomnia. Those things I tended to neglect or ignore when Aggie's needs defined my world finally were able to get a little attention when she was gone. I went to a movie with my husband. I watered the plants. I packed my hospital bag. As we waited for Eldon's arrival, Josh and I spent time together, my mom came down to help, and we all gave extra attention to little Marcus (now 18 months old.) It was a joy to baby the baby who would not be the baby much longer!

What a ridiculous time to have another child. If I had been in complete control of my life's plans, if I could have seen the future, I never would have scheduled a child to be born to me on this day. I never would have planned a pregnancy during the year we moved away from family, the year my firstborn started kindergarten, the year my husband started his new career and I began life as a pastor's wife, and the year seizures would invade our lives. If I had known our family was about to face a trial that would push us far beyond our ability to bear it, one that would systematically destroy each one of my illusions of security, show me how weak I am, and remind me day after day after day how horribly mortal my children and I all are...never, never would I have thought it a good time to open our hearts and home to a fifth child.

Yet my loving Father, who knew all these things, sent us a child anyway. Only God could have made this new life in me, during a year that I found even my own life almost too much to bear. As I look back now, I stand amazed as His wisdom, how He knew exactly what his daughter needed and when, and how He gave one of His greatest gifts to me without even waiting for me to ask. He knew all along, He *knew*, exactly the encouragement my heart needed to make it through this tumultuous year.

April, 2009

Labor and delivery for baby number five was easy and uneventful. When Eldon finally arrived, I praised and thanked God for epidurals once again, and curled up joyfully with my newest little miracle child. My mind had become so cluttered with everything else, I was almost surprised to experience that heart-bursting new-mommy joy. I despise the last weeks of pregnancy, but I absolutely adore the first days of post-partum baby bliss. I love sitting around, inhaling sweet newborn smell, and marveling at God's amazing and adorable handiwork. I love the excuse childbirth provides to take a break from housework and spend long hours sitting on the couch letting a tiny baby sleep on my chest. I love being able to reach my toes again.

I have been through this five times now. Yet, every time, I am surprised at how naturally the newest baby seems to fit into our family. Though I may have worries and anxieties during a pregnancy, when the child arrives it suddenly seems so simple, to again open my heart and welcome yet another one. I love watching my husband, and now my older children, instinctively pour out their own kind of love on the newest child, and I love the delight they experience when the child responds in kind.

The moment of birth is when the baby goes from being "another baby" to *this* baby. No longer knowing him only in general terms, we finally were able to use our arms and hands to welcome and love this particular baby into the family. This child, *Eldon,* is the gift God has given us, and He does know how to give good gifts to His children.

In the coming months, as the trial with Aggie got even worse, baby Eldon was like a living Word from God to my heart. His newborn needs forced me to give him attention, and as I did my eyes were averted from suffering and death to God's most amazing creation of life. Through little baby Eldon, God did not allow sickness, helplessness, or the threat of death to completely blind me to His power and grace.

Though I still had horrible dreams and anxieties about Aggie, the terrors of the night were softened for me when I shared them with Eldon. *He who made this perfect newborn baby is my Father; the God who loves us, Who hears each and every one of our prayers for Aggie.* I enjoyed those few days of refuge, days spent recovering from childbirth and pondering the power and skill of the Father to whom I prayed. *"Our help is in the name of the Lord, who made heaven and earth,"*[5] *and Eldon. Surely, surely the God who made this sweet child could stop Aggie's seizures, or bring some even greater good out of this trial.*

The days of refuge ended well-before I was rested. The three older children returned full of vacation stories and excitement over their new baby brother. The sweet joy of the family reunited was mixed with the bitter reality of the sickness that was tightening its grip on Aggie. She had slipped even further away that week, suffering more frequent "melting" seizures, and becoming less lucid during the times between. Her sunken eyes and exhaustion pierced my heart anew.

Soon it was Eldon's time to receive God's gifts in Baptism. His family's predictable love having already welcomed him into the world, his church family and Heavenly Father did likewise. His gracious Father did not wait until His child was old enough to make up his mind about Him. He created, He sustained, and He immediately welcomed His Eldon into the family. Helpless babies, coming to Him with nothing but need, are welcomed. Children who cannot even walk, much less decide they need God, are carried to Him, and loved into the family by the God that made them.

In Baptism, the baby becomes no longer just "another baby" to the community. God Himself is present, and His entire church gathers to welcome and love this particular baby into God's family. This newborn child of God, *Eldon*, is the gift God has given to all of us. We shared with him God's promises, and we remember that we have been made members of Christ by grace just as this child has.

As Eldon received promises of Life in Christ added to the gracious gift of life and health, my heart also remembered those promises given to the child from whom life was slipping away. In life, in death, there is only One Solid Thing: God's love for us in Christ.

"Fear not, for I have redeemed you. I have called you by name, you are mine." (Isaiah 43:1b)

Chapter 22
Withering

I missed the older children while they were on vacation with their grandparents. I am unsettled any time the family is separated, as if my heart has pieces of it spread out in all different places. When everyone is back together, the pieces of my heart finally are put back where they belong. The family once again is gathered safely under one roof, my heart has been made whole again, and finally, I can rest.

Of course, newborn babies do not allow for much sleep. Eldon turned out to be our fussiest little one to date. I had hoped that baby number five, of sheer necessity, would be a less-demanding kind of baby; but Eldon did not comply with my plans. He knew from day one exactly which way he wanted to sleep, how he had to be held, what texture of blanket he absolutely must have at all times, and a host of other demands that we unsuccessfully attempted to figure out. He was an ornery little fellow, especially during the first few nights.

That did not matter at all to his older brothers and sisters. They were over-the-moon in love with him, especially Lorraine and Seth. While they instinctively knew ways to make him happy, they did not instinctively get his name right. "Eldon" is a bit unusual, and it did not help that they had recently seen the movie "Alvin and the Chipmunks." They called him "Alvin" for awhile, and I even heard little Marcus call him "Elmo" a few times, but eventually, the name "Eldon" stuck.

Marcus slowly realized he was no longer the baby of the family, and he was not happy about it. He ramped up his trouble-making attempts, and often imitated Eldon's cries just for the fun of it, which was not always pleasing to my sleep-deprived ears. He continued to bask in the attention of big sister Lorraine, who began to call him "the second cutest baby in the world." Fortunately, Marcus did not know what "second" meant, he only knew that she still loved him.

We were adjusting to our new baby during that time, and once again, we were adjusting to yet another new kind of Aggie. Aggie's seizures continued to become more frequent and take on new characteristics. She required more supervision, more sleep, and more patience as she exhibited even more odd behavior. She began forgetting words, and had a hard time naming even the most familiar things. She spent more time confused, mentally slippery, and fidgety, and less time able to connect and communicate with those around her.

I missed Aggie while she was gone on vacation, and I continued to miss her, even when she was right next to me. It seemed like each medicine we tried worked the same way: first, slowing the seizures, granting a small reprieve and revival of hope; then, another slipping away, and a falling, each time more deeply, into the abyss of seizures. While I knew we were not yet at the bottom, I was terrified at the downward momentum, and almost panicky as I tried to find some way to stop it.

Once again, we called the doctor, who advised that we stop her latest medicine and try another. The newest medicine did not have as many possible cognitive side effects, but it carried the risk of a rare but life-threatening rash. Because of the rash, she had to receive the medicine very, very gradually. And so, it would take at least nine weeks to know whether or not that particular medicine would be helpful to her. I made it a habit to check her for the rash each night, and tried to set my jaw to endure at least nine more weeks of the storm.

Oh, Father in heaven, please help us know what is best for Aggie. Are we doing enough? Should we get another opinion? Should we try the special diet, look more deeply into surgery, find a way to send her for more tests? Is it time to go to an epilepsy center? Are we just being impatient? Oh, Lord, how I miss her.

We had her records sent to two epilepsy centers for review during this time. We researched, we waited, we prayed, and sometimes we just barely made it through the days. For me, the vibrancy of springtime was nearly overshadowed by one withering flower.

May, 2009

Ever since Aggie was diagnosed with epilepsy in the fall of 2008, there was an undercurrent of sadness in our family that permeated everything we did. Sometimes her struggles were the loudest thing on our minds; sometimes she had good days and we almost forgot about her problems. As we entered May of 2009, the sadness that trickled into our days suddenly turned into a great flood.

Again her seizures changed. Collapsing became more common, seizures lasted several minutes; and in the worst ones, she appeared to hallucinate afterwards. A seizure could slowly reduce her to a limp pile of child on the floor, then suddenly her muscle tone would return, and she would yell, or moan, and flail her arms and legs. Sometimes she would try to run away or hit people, but even if she ran away, we could tell by her eyes that she did not know where she was or what she was doing. We learned that this was actually still part of her seizure, and to keep her safe, attempted to restrain her for several minutes while the seizure ravaged her body. When this kind of seizure finally released its grip on her, she would be utterly exhausted, and seemed to have no memory of the enormous wrestling match that had just occurred.

I remember my husband receiving dirty looks from other parents when she did this at Lowes one afternoon because her fit resembled a temper tantrum. I remember riding out one of these seizures with her in the church office, thankful that her completely unmanageable behavior in the front pew only moments before had caused me to take her out of church. I remember how odd it seemed to let my four year old ride in the stroller that day, and how she almost fell asleep like a baby in the short walk home.

We tried as much as we could to keep our normal commitments during this time, but it was getting much harder. One Monday in May, Josh left for a three-day conference, and I did my best to keep things going at home. The first night he was gone, Eldon had a very difficult first part of the night, giving me no more than ten minutes of sleep at a time. The second part of the night was spent cleaning up Seth's wet bed and coddling an ornery Marcus. I think I got about three hours sleep in all. Because the days were overwhelmed with Aggie's needs, I wondered whether the other children were attempting to get their mommy-time at night!

Tuesday brought another onslaught of problems. Aggie had five wrestling/hallucinating seizures that day, and several small ones in between. When she was not in the grip of a seizure, her behavior was extremely odd. Josh called home to check on us, and decided to come home early from his conference. Almost as soon as he walked in the door, she had yet another four-minute long melting/yelling seizure. After consulting the doctor, we decided it was time to try her emergency medicine: Diastat. Diastat is used for either extremely long seizures that will not stop on their own, or so-called "cluster seizures." Sometimes the brain can "get stuck" having repeated seizures, and Diastat will often "re-set the seizure clock," almost like a computer re-boot. We hoped it would give her some relief.

Giving her Diastat was no small decision. Not only were the side effects scary, but the medicine itself had to be given rectally. It was such an ugly reality, and I hated that her epilepsy was so severe that she needed these drastic measures to give her (we hoped) some kind of relief. I hated that I had to distract the other children from the grim reality of their sister's situation. I got them settled with various activities in other rooms, and Josh and I called Aggie.

"Come here, Princess," he said, gently lifting her into her Tinkerbell bed. The canopies still flowed gracefully down over each little girl's bed, and they gave the entire room an enchanted and magical feel. What a great place for sweet, little-girl dreams, childhood memories, innocence and beauty. Her daddy called her "Princess" before we administered the rectal medicine that would stop her relentless seizures, and it all seemed so cruel. No four-year-old princess should have to endure this. No childhood bedroom should be filled with these awful images and the threat of death.

After the next wrestling match ended, Aggie relaxed, and the medicine took effect. She was snoring in a matter of minutes, and I curled up next to her in her bed. I was grateful Josh was home to look after the other children so that I could just be with her. Sure, I had to watch for side effects, but I also needed so badly to be near her, to see her at peace, if only for a short time. *How long, Lord?*

Chapter 23
Just Breathe

**"I have set the LORD always before me;
because he is at my right hand,
I shall not be shaken.
Therefore my heart is glad
and my whole being rejoices;
my flesh also dwells secure."
(Psalm 16:8-9)**

The Diastat kept Aggie's seizures completely away for two more days, sixty hours in all. Like the anesthesia used for MRIs, this medicine also caused extreme behavior changes. Aggie was uncoordinated and wild. She ran through the house, tripping over things, starting wrestling matches, and injuring herself and others repeatedly. She was very difficult to manage, but at least she had a small break from seizures. As the medicine wore off, the grip of epilepsy took hold again, and in no time at all she was back to the worst we had ever seen her.

One afternoon, the girls and I were returning from the park, walking down a small hill in the parking lot on the way back to the house. Lorraine and Aggie ran off ahead, but at the top of the hill I saw Aggie stop and look to the side, as a seizure began to take hold of her. I ran to catch up to her and stood by her while she slowly slumped to the ground. "It's ok, Lorraine, she's having a seizure. You go on ahead. We'll head home in a minute." Aggie's limp body lay on my lap. I gently set her head on my leg so that I could stroke her hair while we waited for the seizure to pass.

Wow, this one seems to be taking a long time, I thought as I began to get a little uncomfortable on the hard ground. I brushed back her hair one more time then turned her face towards me to see whether there was any sign of awareness coming back into her eyes. The image that assaulted my eyes in that moment is one I will never forget. Her eyes were sunken and blank, her face had no expression whatsoever. Her skin had turned completely ashen, and her lips were dark blue. I held her mouth to my ear to confirm my fear: she was not breathing!

"Lorraine!!!" I yelled, "Go get your daddy!" I scooped her up, her pale face and blue lips pointed towards the sky, and her head bounced along as I attempted to run with her. I was panicking, thinking somehow, if I just got her home, Josh would know what to do.

I ran with her for just a few steps when all of a sudden she was back. Color poured into her face, her eyes met mine, and she was once again breathing. "It's okay, Lorraine, she's fine," I panted. "Why don't you head back home and we will catch up to you in a minute." Aggie was back, but extremely tired, and in no hurry to get home. Neither was I. My shaking legs lowered us both to back to the ground. We sat on the concrete while I stroked her hair and rocked her back and forth, and I wondered where all of this was headed.

May 11, 2009

This trial with Aggie seems to be only beginning, Lord. Your faithfulness has carried us this far. Lord, continue to be my strength. You know what I wrestle with. I thought she died in my arms today. Her blue lips and ashen face and no breath...oh, Lord, how that image haunts me. Is that how it will end, Lord? In five years? This afternoon? Death seems so close, like it is teasing and taunting me.

The days following the first seizure that took away Aggie's breath reminded me of my more difficult postpartum experiences. Though I never faced weeks or months of depression, I did have some extremely dark days after having children. I remember irritability, feeling overwhelmed, irrational sadness, and fatigue. Those were difficulties, to be sure, but the teasing and taunting of Death was by far the worst. Sometimes I would have horrible, violent dreams that were nearly impossible to shake even in the daylight. Other times, normal mommy-anxiety would turn into something similar. The flutter every mother feels when her child is trying something new on the monkey bars, or goofing off at the top of a slide, seemed to stimulate a host of nasty images in my brain. On my bad days, the anxiety that elicits the uncontrollable "Honey, be careful!" would be accompanied by an extremely vivid flash of what could happen, right down to the bloody skull, the hospital beds, and the child-sized coffin. Injected into that mental vision were all of the awful emotions that would accompany the reality, and those feelings would linger long after I forced the pictures far from my mind. On those bad days, I simply could not shake the awful sense that everything around me was horrifically fragile, decaying, and dying.

I know Christ is risen, and I do believe and trust His promises. Yet, God knows my weakness, my immaturity. He knows that I hate the thought of death. I do not welcome it, and most of the time I want to pretend it will never happen to me or anyone I love. I do not like the fact that we can see the church cemetery from our home, because sometimes when I see it I wonder whether I will ever have to bury a child there.

To survive those post-partum days, I learned quickly that my only hope was to remember the Lord. There was no escape from the reality. We are mortal, but Christ is risen. As I look back, I suspect those nasty experiences may have been a sort of training exercise for the reality I faced that year with Aggie. When Aggie was sick, Death's harassment no longer was going on merely in my head. Threats to Aggie were everywhere, and most of my fears for her were rational. There was no place without some sort of safety concern, and even if those were minimal, the threats from the seizures themselves were becoming much more serious. *Will a seizure take away her breath for good?* I constantly was asking the Lord this question, and receiving no answer. She fluttered around at the edge of a cliff, and any moment she might fall away into eternity.

Yet, Lord, she did take another breath, and she is here with us today. And for every nasty image of sickness I have another image of life and joy with my dear Aggie: like her huge smile and happy piggy tails and giddy shoulders as she sat next to her daddy in the front of church yesterday during the children's sermon.

There are some thoughts that I am only now daring to think, that my mind is still trying to comprehend:

My child may deteriorate mentally before my eyes and never get better.

My child could die in my arms today, or in her sleep tonight.

My illusions of security are quickly falling away.

Oh, Jesus, hold me close.

Simply putting Aggie to bed at night became an enormous exercise of faith for me. I knew in my mind that my concern for Aggie was powerless to sustain her life; but still, I wanted to keep her in my arms at all times, to try somehow to love away her problems. To allow her to sleep in her own bed, and to go to bed myself, was tremendously difficult and would not have been possible without God's help. Through His Word and the encouragement of others, He gently, repeatedly pointed me back to the reality of His love. *Yes, death's threats are everywhere, and death may even take this child of your heart this very night. You no longer can close your eyes to this, daughter. Yet there is great comfort to be found, even in this valley of death. Death would only take her from your care into Mine. Lean on me, daughter, I am faithful and My promises do not fail.*

My grip on reality was fickle at times, but Reality had His grip on me, and so I was not allowed to fall. Scripture was my food and my air, the one thing I could trust when everything around me seemed to be decaying. As I stood with my church family each Sunday, I held tightly to every Word of Scripture, the creeds, and the hymns. God's Truth was my solid rock, my security in a world that was falling to pieces. So that I would survive, I carved out time to soak in the truth, listen to old hymns, and burn Scripture on my mind. I began to post God's Words of encouragement to me around the house, knowing that on some days it would be difficult for me even to get from one room to the next without losing my way.

God helped me loosen my grip on Aggie, just a little. She was a gift from God, on loan to us for as long as He chose. I could not help but wonder each evening whether, this time, "goodnight" would mean "goodbye." Yet I knew I had no choice but to commit her to His loving care. His power threatened my strongest desires, yet His Word became my comfort, and I posted this verse right above her bed:

"In peace I will both lie down and sleep; for you alone, O LORD, make me dwell in safety." (Psalm 4:8)

Chapter 24
Joy

Aggie's rapid decline even after the emergency medicine, combined with the new breath-stealing seizures, earned her an emergency appointment with her neurologist. Her doctor gave us a large amount of time and agreed that it was time to become more aggressive in her treatment. It may seem that I was slow to understand, but only at this point was I beginning to understand that not only did my daughter have epilepsy, she had *severe* epilepsy.

Though we all were beginning to suspect that medicine would not be her answer, her doctor recommended that we try one more of what he called "the big guns." Bigger guns cause more damage of course, so the potential side effects were intimidating. Yet it was obvious at this point that it was necessary to risk liver damage and so forth if there was any hope of stopping these awful seizures before they consumed her completely.

Her doctor agreed that it was time to seek more intensive testing at an epilepsy center, so we began to make arrangements. We looked forward to the team approach at an epilepsy center, and hoped that the bright medical minds we would meet there would have some good news for our Aggie. It was time to do something radical if we could, be it surgery, or an extremely restrictive diet, or anything at all. *Please, God, anything, other than continuing down this road we are on.* We did not have a quick fix, but we returned home with a little more hope for her, and began setting our faces for Cleveland Clinic.

I began to redefine what I called "good days," no longer basing the quality on the number of seizures, but on the intensity of death's harassment. Seizures that affected her breathing never became easy to watch, for each time I was certain that she would never breathe again. Yet she had days without that kind of seizures, and some small pieces of normal life remained.

⚜

We own a ridiculous but terrific children's video called "Hide 'Em in Your Heart." It is simply a collection of Bible verses put to music with children acting them out. My children love it, despite the fact that it was produced in the 1980's. By letting them watch it, I risk letting them grow up thinking big hair and red jeans are normal, but the songs make it worth that risk. One day, we were watching that video when Aggie's favorite song came on: "A joyful heart is good medicine, but a broken spirit dries up the bones." (Proverbs 17:22) This song is one of the silliest ones, and includes a dancing clown that cheers up a child in the hospital. Typically, Aggie cannot restrain herself when this song is on, and her dancing usually overflows into a family dance party.

I sat next to her on the couch when this song started. She had just had a few small seizures in a row. When she heard the beginning of the song, her eyes lit up and she turned her face towards the television. But as she sat there, it was as if her brain could not keep up with the words of the song so that she could sing. Dancing was out of the question. She stared vaguely at the screen for a few minutes, then mentally drifted off into space.

As I saw that happening I felt the grief welling up again; but as I sat there with Aggie, I felt the Lord encouraging me with His Word. Aggie had always been a playful joy-bringer, ever since she was a baby, and it was hard to see her joyless. *But the words are still true: "A joyful heart is good medicine." My little joy-bringer needs a rest, but that did not mean there could be no joy. Perhaps,* I thought, *the joy and energy that normally come from her can encourage her when it comes from other people.*

As I thought of this, I realized I had seen this happen many times already. When Daddy came home each day, all the children would get excited; but Aggie always would drop whatever it was she was doing to run with all her might to greet him, giving him the biggest hug she could muster. What a blessing that he had the energy to tease and play with the children, even when Aggie was sick. God also provided fresh energy through the junior high girls from school, and from our friend and neighbor Mary Anne. I began accepting their offers to help out of sheer necessity, just so I could get bills paid and other things done, and only later did I realize what a blessing their energy was for the children.

Lord, help me be a joy-bringer to my little girl today. Thank you for all the others you have sent into our lives to care for this family during this time, bringing us food and encouragement, playfulness and joy. As we all walk with Aggie through this valley, may we continue to remember Your promises and Your love for us that allow us to "rejoice always."

When circumstances did not create a mood of happiness in our home, God sent us other reasons for joy and kept holding onto us. I am so glad that God heard my cries and did not get tired of my requests for strength, patience, safety for Aggie, and help of all kinds. And as the concerned people in our new church family showed us, when one of His members is hurting, everyone hurts. Aggie was a child of God, a member of His family, not just ours. Our new home happened to be one of those precious, rare places that still functions as a truly caring community. We may have been way down at the end of our rope, but we were definitely cared for down there!

There were moments of green pastures and still waters, even in this dark season. One weekend we went with Josh's parents to the state park, and that small outing turned out to be an amazingly refreshing day for all of us. Aggie was more like herself than she had been in a very long time, and for a brief moment, I could stop missing her and just enjoy her. She had only mild seizures, and mostly spent the day flitting around like a hummingbird with her huge Aggie-smile on her face. It was "just" a normal, uneventful spring day at the park, but this time my eyes could see what a gift it was. It was a blessing of enormous value to our weary family.

Could this be the new medicine kicking in or was it just a good day? Will the medicine keep working next week if it works this week? I don't know, and I almost want to guard against hope for fear of disappointment. But that is not right either, is it? Hold me constantly, and help me keep on doing what is in front of me. There is enough work and worry to keep me busy today. But on this day, there is also a joyful Aggie to flutter around with me.

Thank You, Lord, for that uneventful, normal day. My heart needed that.

Chapter 25
Just Fine

After a few good days with Aggie on the latest medicine, she went back to square one. Her apneic seizures returned, and she had two in one day, along with thirteen other seizures. We again resorted to Diastat, and exchanged the seizures for a day of dopey behavior and confusion. The doctor said this medicine could be used up to twice per week if necessary. It was not a good long term strategy, but we knew it might be necessary until we could get her to an epilepsy center. We finally received a firm date from Cleveland Clinic: July 7.

I stumbled on a Scripture passage that week that was both disturbing and comforting to me:
"As he passed by, he saw a man blind from birth. And his disciples asked him, 'Rabbi, who sinned, this man or his parents, that he was born blind?'
Jesus answered, 'It was not that this man sinned, or his parents, but that the works of God might be displayed in him.'" (John 9:1-3)

It was a comfort to know that suffering did not necessarily mean that God was unhappy with us about something we did. It was also a bit unsettling. If we had been doing something wrong, there might be hope that we could figure out what it was and fix it, and everything would be okay again. If the reason for this trial had nothing to do with us but rather with some unknown plan of God, well, that is pretty frightening. I actually was quite comfortable imagining that I had control over where our life was headed, over what kind of family we would be. It was hard to let go of that illusion.

June 2009

You know my heart, Lord: I do not want to be made an example of! Nor do I want Aggie to be if it means suffering! I want a comfortable, normal life that I can pretty much control! If You are the One with the master plan, then that means I have no idea where this is heading. Forgive me, Lord. I am scared to trust You with her...but I have no other choice. You promise to do all things for the good of Your children. You are her Father and You love her more than we do; Your Word tells us so. Display your works in her, Lord, in us, if you must. But please, Jesus, give us glimpses of it now and then!

It was a relief to finally have a date on the calendar for the epilepsy center. The more we learned about Cleveland Clinic, the more our hope for Aggie revived. She would spend at least three days undergoing tests: another MRI, video EEG, neuro-psychological testing, and a PET scan to investigate metabolic problems. We hoped all these things would give us a clearer understanding of what was happening to Aggie.

We were beginning to fear that medicine would not be the answer for Aggie, but there were other possibilities. As horrible as brain surgery once sounded to me, it was now less awful than the reality we were facing without it. From our research, we learned that brain surgery was only an option for people with a specific "seizure focus," that is, a part of the brain that seemed to be causing the seizures. If they could find a focus (perhaps the spot that showed up on her MRI), and if that focus was reachable without causing too many other problems, then she would be a candidate for surgery. Even surgery was not a guarantee. Seventy percent of patients with refractory epilepsy (not controlled with medicine) are seizure-free after surgery. If she was not a candidate for surgery, there were other options to explore as well, like the ketogenic diet and vagus nerve stimulation.

We expected Cleveland to be a time of big decisions. How does a person prepare for something like that? How do you get ready for hope, risk, and enormous decisions? Would Aggie be coming home with us? The same Aggie we took? A helped Aggie? A brain-damaged Aggie? Would we come back with good news and hope, or devastating news and last resorts? We did not know, so we just kept on doing what was in front of us, holding on to the Lord, and hugging all of the kids a little tighter along the way.

Although Aggie had been having seizures for almost nine months at this point, there was still a bit of unreality to the entire situation for me. Some days I felt like my eyes were open to the situation, I assessed problems objectively, and I handled them the best I could. Other days were more of a struggle, especially when we were forced to consider doing something new to adapt to her disability, considering another risky drug, or talking about brain surgery. I could go through the motions for a time, but before long I would begin to fight the whole situation, and my heart would cry out, "WAIT just a minute! Are we really talking about brain surgery here? She was just fine!"

Sometimes it was very small things that produced this reaction in me. As her seizures progressed during spring and summer, Aggie at times became incredibly oral. She would constantly lick or chew on everything, and I mean everything: her shirt, her hair, toys, rocks at the park, paper, everything! It was weird, it was gross, and it had the potential to drive me bonkers. Apparently, this is a common behavior for someone with epilepsy in the temporal lobe, as hers seemed to be. Apparently, it was probably more of a compulsive need than a trainable discipline issue. Apparently, somebody makes safe chewy necklaces that children can wear for this purpose. *Now wait just a minute, are we really talking about my four-year-old princess wearing a slobbery necklace all the time? Hold on, she's really not that bad, and it's not all the time, and she was JUST fine! Just five minutes ago...okay, last fall.* It still felt like I just turned my head for one minute, I looked away when she was fine and all of a sudden she was not. I still was partly expecting things to snap right back to normal if we just waited, just a few more minutes...just a few more.

I suppose these are the same kinds of feelings people experience after a loved one dies suddenly or someone gets a nasty diagnosis. We stare in shock and amazement, stammering, "He was just fine...how can this be?"

Death and sickness are everywhere in this fallen world, and yet we always are so shocked when they come near us. Why is that? We feel good at this very moment, so we expect to tonight, and tomorrow, and a few years from now. We are receiving life in full measure at this very moment, by pure grace, and because we have been given it right now, we assume it is ours to keep forever. Our babies are born to us healthy and we expect them to stay that way.

Then in a moment things change. Our eyes are opened, and we see how fragile we are. We try desperately to close our eyes again, to return to that sweet, safe dream.

But there is no safety at all, absolutely none, other than in the hands of our God.

Other refuge I have none;
hangs my helpless soul on Thee.
Leave, ah leave, me not alone,
Still support and comfort me!
All my trust on Thee is stayed,
All my help from Thee I bring;
Cover my defenseless head
With the shadow of Thy wing.[6]

Chapter 26
Loving this Aggie

God gave us some rest before our trip to Cleveland. We spent time with both sides of the family in Michigan, sharing with them the strange mixture of deep grief and abundant joy that had become our way of life that summer.

Seth and Marcus both hit a stage I call "I-wonder-what-will-happen-if-I..." They spent most of their summer time creatively wondering, experimenting, and facing consequences of said experiments.

Seth: *I wonder what would happen if I tried to drive my Grandpa's golf cart? I wonder whether he will figure out who crashed it?*

Marcus: *I wonder what sound Eldon makes when I poke him right here? How about here? Here? How many times can I poke him before Mommy chases me away?*

Seth: *I wonder what would happen if I drank a bottle of bubbles?*

Marcus: *I wonder what would happen if I laughed about getting a spanking?*

Seth: *I wonder what would happen if I looked right at Daddy and smiled while dumping my lemonade out on the table?*

Marcus: *I wonder what would happen if I tried to eat a rock? A piece of chalk? A bug? My shoe? My sister?*

Seth: *I wonder what would happen if I ran home ahead of my baby-sitter (since she is slowed down by a screaming, hungry baby) and then locked the door on her? I wonder what would happen if I danced around and laughed instead of letting her in?*

I often wondered what would happen if I ran into the woods and hid for a few days, but I never did try it.

Instead of hiding, I did the best I could to engage in the little joys of our young children. Vacation Bible School always has been something I look forward to in the summer. While I usually liked to help, I stayed out of this first VBS at our new church and focused on managing my own children, especially Aggie. I remembered the previous year, at our small church in Michigan, how both girls thrived in that setting, throwing themselves into the action and coming home exhausted.

We still came home exhausted that year, but I was exhausted for unpleasant reasons. It was hard to believe how much had changed in one year. *Last year Aggie thrived in that situation. She participated. She made friends. She loved every second of it. She was not the problem-child in the room. She did not require one-on-one care. She did not get distracted from the Bible stories by a compulsive need to eat a sticker.*

She had a few lucid moments, for which I was grateful, but I was beginning to realize that some of her behaviors had become simply unmanageable. They no longer were merely difficult, they were impossible. No amount of training or preparation or discipline will help with behaviors over which a child has no control.. Some things we just survived, and when that became too tough or too disruptive, we just went home.

Those little things, things other people hardly noticed, were breaking my heart. Yes, all kids have a few quirks, but this was different. Sure, other kids have trouble listening. Other kids put odd things in their mouths. Other kids feel anti-social at times. Other kids like to climb on everything and wash their hands with toothpaste (all right, maybe not that last one). But when I saw Aggie doing those things, I knew it was somehow *not her.* It was the epilepsy, or the drugs, or both. It was the *problem,* reaching into her tiny little head and changing everything around, confusing her and all of us, making her think and do things she normally would not.

Part of me still waited for her to just *snap out of it already!* Yet my husband gently insisted, "The Aggie we knew before epilepsy is gone." I hated that thought, I fought against it, and I despised every bit of evidence that proved it true.

I remember talking one night with Josh and his mother about the changes we saw in Aggie over the past year. We were remembering the way Aggie once loved interacting with others and thrived in social situations, they way she lit up a room and brought even more life to any activity. We noted how drastically different she had become, how she seemed to prefer, on most occasions, to be left alone. Grandma said, "That's how she is now and that's okay."

I did not want to accept that, and felt both angry and sad as I considered it; but I slowly was starting to see that it was true. My memories of the way she once was would always be dear to me, but I was not helping her by constantly fighting the person she had become.

I loved Aggie. I loved the Aggie I knew, the one I gave birth to while Daddy was in Iraq, the one who loved starting parties and having fun and teasing and drinking chocolate milk. Now and then I saw glimpses of that Aggie, though most of the time I found myself taking care of other Aggies: wild-and-out-of-control Aggie, tired-and-pathetic Aggie, confused

Aggie, drunk-and-happy Aggie, antisocial Aggie, and emotionally fragile Aggie, just to name a few.

As I thought of these things one evening, a ridiculous song popped into my head: "If you can't be with the one you love, Honey, love the one you're with!" It made me laugh, and though I know the songwriter was speaking to an entirely different situation, the general idea seemed to be just what I needed to learn. My prayers changed slightly, and though I never stopped begging God to restore Aggie to herself, I began to pray also that He teach me how to love her in whatever form she appeared.

As summer came, I found myself beginning to accept some of the extra work I was required to do to care for the daughter I had. It was not undue mommy-anxiety I was fighting. Accidents were going to happen, and they really could cause serious injury or even death. So, if I was going to allow her to do risky things, like leave her bedroom, I had to make the commitment to stay close by to watch her constantly. As I had my morning coffee and prayer time, I often gave myself a pep talk that went something like this:

Today Aggie will have seizures. Today Aggie will require extra-ordinary supervision, mind-alerting drugs, and emergency preparedness plans. Today my attention will be divided, and the other children will not get everything they want. Today my seizure antenna will be on high power, and my feet will always be ready to catch her when (not if) she falls. Today, if we go out in public, we will risk embarrassment and injury. Today letting her "be a kid" will come with anxiety and constant supervision. Today we must live with epilepsy.

Lord, please give me what I need to do this job today, and keep working on that better plan for tomorrow! I have prayed a million times for You to fix Aggie, yet the storm rages on. Your thoughts and Your plans are bigger than mine. Help me to trust You through this trial. I see changes in Aggie that break my heart. But the fact is, this unpredictable, changing Aggie is the one I am called to love and to serve. Lord make my heart bigger, help me adapt to her new needs, help me to accept where she is right now and love her as she needs to be loved today. In Jesus' name, Amen.

Chapter 27
Provision

Life still was exhausting and unpredictable, but there was a certain kind of freedom in allowing myself to simply love whatever form of Aggie happened to be near me. We stayed closer to home and simply endured those days, always looking forward with hope to her appointment at Cleveland Clinic Epilepsy Center. Because we had not yet exhausted all options, we could not afford too much acceptance at this stage, for Aggie's sake. Josh and I were resolved to fight for her, to be her advocates, and to do everything we could to get her the best help available. I would love the Aggie I had with me each day, but I would not completely let go of the Aggie she once was. Not yet.

Loving Aggie was complicated and painful, and I never did find a way to balance all the contradictions. My heart was always in knots with conflicts: the acceptance of trials wrestled the resolve to fight; the smothering protection wrestled the desire to let her take risks; the possessive "love" that attempted to will away all her problems wrestled resignation to God's mysterious will. Sin stained all these things in my heart, and I was powerless to untangle the mess. Yet even though He could see all of this mess, my Heavenly Father held me close. God was faithful, and He never once failed to provide.

I did not always feel like He was providing. Many of the things I thought I desperately needed in those days were things I never did receive. I wanted Aggie better of course, but if that was not going to happen, I still had a long list of other things I thought I needed to survive. I wanted extra energy. I wanted nerves of steel. I wanted a baby who would sleep at night. I wanted absolutely no other little problems to invade my world. I wanted older children who did not fight. I wanted mental peace despite the chaos around me. I wanted patience. I wanted unshakable confidence in God and His plan. I wanted to know we were going to survive this. I wanted uninterrupted nap time. I wanted, at the very least, to look like I was strong.

Yet problems continued to bombard, and instead of getting stronger, I felt myself getting weaker. My heart was selfish and sinful, my flesh was weak, and my dear baby was not getting better. She had more seizures that took away her breath; that sucked the color out of her body and turned her lips blue. Death's cold hand grabbed her, often right from my arms, and I watched helplessly as life was drained from her. When I was certain it had been drained completely, certain her heart had stopped, and certain my own heart never would recover, life suddenly would flood through her again. Yet I sensed Death lurking around every corner, taunting and harassing; and I never knew when he would strike his final blow.

God did not give me super-human strength to survive those awful days. But in this season of sadness and pain, God knew that my greatest need was to be reminded of His grace and goodness. *"Believe, and trust!"* I would encourage myself. *"Trust Him and His goodness...despite all evidence to the contrary,"* my sinful self quipped. I tried to cling to Truth, telling myself that God loves us and He has a plan in all of this. My eyes strained to see a glimpse of that plan every day, but I could see only sadness and pain. Death and sickness harassed Aggie while sin, doubt, and despair harassed me.

During this dark and cold time, God had mercy on my weakness and sent me encouragement in every form. Every hug from my husband, every meal, every phone call, every offer of help, I received as a gentle reminder from God Himself that we had not been forsaken. Though He refused to answer the biggest cries of my heart, the smaller gifts carried some consolation. He *is* good. He reminded me, relentlessly, through acts of kindness from His children.

My aunt, whose heart constantly shared our trials, encouraged me in many ways as she related her own experiences:

" I also didn't have the strength at the time. I don't think I have it now. What you and I do have is a God who meets us where we are and helps us navigate the 'unknowns' in life. I have found that in my weakest times He has brought people around me to help me and my family get through the situation. Sometimes it is just Him and me. I now have some deep friendships and a deeper relationship with Him from those times. It's okay not to be able to 'handle it.' Allow Him and the people He has brought into your life to help you get through it."

As my aunt showed me, sometimes leaning on God means leaning on those God sends to us. Though it was uncomfortable at times, I often had no other choice. I hated crying in front of other people. I still do. I remember one day at the mom's group when my tears came out of nowhere and I could not stop them. I do not recall a single thing anybody said that day, but I do remember the sympathy, the prayers, and the unconditional support. As another friend wrote, "I remember what it feels like to long for normal so much, it's excruciating…No one knows what to say or do, but I hope you can feel the love and support all around you as your friends stand by your side and wait with you."

Praise be to God, that even though my heart was fraught with darkness and unbelief, I never was forsaken. I felt His children standing beside us, ready to help, praying, and waiting with us. I saw them, and through them I saw Him. God knows His children are weak, and He knows that we need Him to be even more persistent than the enemy. He was that to me. He ignored my silly requests for sleep and nerves of steel, and pursued me instead with the great gift of Himself. His Word, His Sacraments, and each gift of encouragement given though His children were like cords that wrapped around me. As all other things I thought I could trust were crumbling, His cords held me fast and drew me ever closer to Him.

Who shall separate us from the love of Christ? Shall tribulation, or distress, or persecution, or famine, or nakedness, or danger, or sword? As it is written, 'For your sake we are being killed all the day long; we are regarded as sheep to be slaughtered.' No, in all these things we are more than conquerors through him who loved us. For I am sure that neither death nor life, nor angels nor rulers, nor things present nor things to come, nor powers, nor height nor depth, nor anything else in all creation, will be able to separate us from the love of God in Christ Jesus our Lord. (Romans 8:35-39)

Chapter 28
The Epilepsy Center

July, 2009

Finally, the days of merely enduring were over, and it was time to go to Cleveland. Josh and I left Lorraine, Seth and Marcus in the loving care of grandparents, and set off with Aggie and Eldon. We began our journey fortified by the love and prayers of others, and carrying a determination to do anything, to try anything, if it could help Aggie be Aggie again. *Jesus, go before us!*

As Josh drove, the children slept and I prayed:

Lord, I am surprised at the peace I feel at this moment—this must be from You. It is going to be such a week of stress: the actual tests performed on our little Aggie, and then the results (worse than that, the in-between while we wait for results). This week could completely change our lives—in a wonderful way, if we find amazing help—or for worse. A terrible diagnosis is possible, as is a seizure from which she does not recover, if they take her off medicine during testing. What kind of Aggie will we bring home with us?

Lord, You are teaching me to pray for daily bread, to ask for strength and patience for this moment, and not try to bear now those things that may be in my future. My job is to live and love and serve in this moment, leaning on You now. Really, most of my present moments are enough to occupy my time and prayer life completely. Fruitless worry about the future actually steals my attention from the present where I am needed. It is here in the present that You meet me and provide for me.

Anxiety and fear are part of my cross in this moment, but they are just feelings. I am not called to bear the actual things I am anxious or fearful about—yet. Help me through this day of anxiety and fear; let the fruits of the Spirit not die in me because of those mere feelings.

Aggie had been told that we were taking her to a hospital for testing, but she cared little. When she was awake, she was fully occupied with her books and toys. We noticed her seizure pattern changing once again. Every hour or two she would have either a long nasty seizure or a cluster of 6-10 very short seizures, sometimes immediately followed by a severe seizure. I had begun to keep her emergency medicine very close at hand. By this time, she needed Diastat at least once per week. It seemed to pull her back from the brink of death each time, but it also was losing its effectiveness. The dosage that once stopped seizures for sixty hours now worked for only nine.

The morning before her first appointment, Aggie was sitting at the table in the hotel room, playing a computer game, as I sat on the couch with Eldon. A seizure made her pause and look up into the distance. I stayed where I was and watched her go in and out of a seizure about ten times, as was normal for her that week. Then the seizures quit harassing her, and she quietly returned to frosting and decorating digital cakes. I resumed dressing the baby, turning my back to her, assuming she was "safe" from seizures for another hour or two. A minute later, I noticed the chatter of the game had ceased again. I looked up, and there was Aggie, her cheek smushed on the table, staring blankly ahead, with her hand still on the mouse. I jumped up, watching her head slide slowly as her entire body became weak. Before I could reach her, her head slipped off the table and plummeted directly to the floor, her limp body following behind.

I sat on the floor and cuddled my sad, little rag doll, releasing one more time some tears and grief before we faced the day. *It is time for drastic measures. There is no doubt in my mind.*

Cleveland Clinic is enormous, like a city in itself. It was huge, well-organized, and full of activity. Our small, sick daughter was welcomed into a fortress of healing, where soldiers of medicine would mobilize on her behalf. Like the children's hospital in Indiana, this hospital was bursting with sad people and sick children, but I no longer pretended I was not part of that club. I clung to hope, thinking, *surely, in a massive place like this, there must be an answer for my baby.*

Her first appointment was with an epileptologist. A small, friendly woman burst into the room and introduced herself to Aggie and to us. Though she was petite, her presence completely filled the room. She immediately went to work, asking a million questions about the type, frequency, and changes in Aggie's seizure pattern. I gave her the records I had been keeping, relieved that someone cared about the details. She gave Aggie a physical exam and even observed a seizure. She noticed small details we had missed, most notably, slight motor impairment on her right side. Aggie was unable to hop on her right foot. The doctor spent over an hour with us, collecting data and explaining what we could expect next. She eagerly consumed all information about Aggie's condition, and we hardly could wait until she had time to digest it. Though we could not yet see how the pieces fit together, her demeanor made me confident that there were answers, and that she would find them.

Medicine is typically the first treatment for seizures. Obviously, Aggie's were not responding, so it was time to explore the next step: surgery. As the doctor explained, there are three questions to be answered when considering brain surgery for epilepsy.

Is it warranted? (The doctor spoke in tune with my heart: her epilepsy was obviously severe. The answer to that question was most definitely "yes.")

Is surgery possible? (Will it work?)

Is it safe? (Where is the trouble spot in the brain in relation to other important functions?)

She outlined the action plan for the tests that would help answer the remaining questions. She then gave us a printed record of our meeting with her, and directed us to our next appointment. As we left, she said, "I am glad you are here. I think we can help your daughter." *What sweet, beautiful words!*

∽✖∾

Aggie was a most cooperative patient during her various appointments. She showed no concern about any of the things we were discussing, and was mostly content to color or watch movies during the waiting periods between appointments. The difficult parts for her were still to come: the IV poke for MRI sedation, the application of the EEG leads, the blood draws. She knew this on some level, but she seemed incapable of worry. As she skipped out of the epileptologist's office she entertained us and all of the people in the waiting room with several rounds of "Zip-a-Dee-Doo-Dah!"

She waited quietly for her MRI, where we were pleased to find they used gas instead of IV sedation. After she recovered from that, we found the epilepsy floor and got her settled there. It was time to begin the long EEG and observation period.

When he came to apply the EEG leads, the technician said the procedure should not cause her any pain. The leads would have to stay put for one to three days, until the doctors had enough information, so they used a different technique to apply them. They drew on her head, then applied glue and the leads, and used an air gun to quickly dry the glue. Something about the procedure made the poor girl absolutely bonkers. She screamed bloody murder for a good half hour until she wore herself out with exhaustion.

Of course, I hated watching her scream, and even though they said it should not hurt, there is still something horrible about watching your child scream like that while someone repeatedly pokes her in the head with an air gun that looked like an enormous needle. At one point, Eldon began screaming along with her so I took him into the hallway. He cheered up, but she continued to scream; and I wondered how much of this we all could take.

As much as we tried to convince her that fighting was futile, she continued to fight for all she was worth. Every IV poke, every blood draw was an enormous battle during her entire time at the Clinic. Like her, I made pathetic attempts to avoid pain during this whole situation as well, through distraction, stoic resolve, or denial. My attempts were just as silly and futile. Love makes people vulnerable. Love opens us up to both joy and pain, and when a loved one suffers, sometimes it seems like love is nothing but pain. I could not love Aggie without hurting myself, yet I could not help but love her.

I prayed for strength each day to my God who understood this completely, who made Himself vulnerable in His love for me, even to the point of death on a cross.

"The Lord is near to the brokenhearted, and saves the crushed in spirit." (Psalm 34:18)

Chapter 29
Something to Try

The days Aggie spent hooked up to the EEG were filled with plenty of seizure activity. Josh and I were told to push the help button any time she had a seizure so that the event would be set apart from the mounds of data being recorded, and so that the nurses could observe and help if needed. We dutifully observed Aggie, as we always did, and pushed the button every hour or two. This was habit for me: observe and take note, observe and take note, observe and take note. Every time we pushed the button two to five people came rushing in to observe her seizure. It was so strange to me to have such a production made of every little seizure. Yet in some ways, it was a relief to have so many others there to help keep her safe. I was comforted by the nurses armed with Diastat who ran to her bedside several times a day.

Though she kept the staff very busy, Aggie also kept them smiling. I remember one night, when a new nurse came in to introduce herself. She approached Aggie's bed, but before she could say a word Aggie smiled and said, "I'm called Aggie."

"Well, hi there, Aggie. I'm called Elaine. Queen Elaine. Are you Princess Aggie?"

Aggie became very serious. "No." she insisted. "I am called Aggie…. and I'm Peter Pan!"

"Oh, well it's nice to meet you, Aggie Peter Pan!"

"I'm Aggie Sue Cook. Aggie Peter Pan. Aggie Sue Cook Peter Pan." She smiled her big Aggie smile at her twentieth new friend that day. She then introduced the nurse to her mom and dad, her baby brother, her froggy, her Peter Pan, her Curious George, her brand new Dr. Bear, and her Teddy Bear blanket.

Each day, the epileptologist and her team made the rounds on the epilepsy floor. Each time Aggie's doctor came to see us, her presence filled the room entirely. Surrounded by her team, she seemed even more powerful. She spoke with us, with Aggie, and with the team, succinctly summarizing all the information and charting the next course of action. If she needed another test or another piece of information, she dispatched one of her assistants, and considered it done. She had command of a small army of medical professionals. As she sent each of these on various errands, I could almost imagine her taking similar command of the moon and the stars, simply waving her hand and bidding them to do her will. Surely epilepsy was no match for this woman.

After almost two days of testing, the team was ready to advise. "Her epilepsy is coming from all over," the doctor explained, confirming our fears. Typically when there is no clear-cut seizure focus, epilepsy surgery is not an option. But Aggie's doctor was not bound by what is "typical" in her field of expertise. "Although we do not see a clear focus, that abnormality in her brain is still a possible culprit," she explained. Surgery still seemed like the logical next step, though she could not promise it would solve the problem. Yet, she reasoned, "We have seen too much success in these kinds of cases not to give it a try. It is probably a tumor, and it *may* help to take it out."

Although we would rather have had a guaranteed solution than just another thing to "try," we immediately began making plans for surgery. My greatest fear was no longer surgery; rather, it was exhausting all options, hearing those horrible words, "There is nothing else we can do for her." As awful as she looked, lying glassy-eyed in her hospital bed, she still had options, and we had no choice but to pursue the next thing.

July 9, 2009

Lord, you have sustained us through this trial at the Clinic so far. You have provided excellent doctors and nurses, and (thank you!) a crystal clear next step: brain surgery. Aggie has a tumor, and it must come out. Probably next week.

Lord, thank you that there is something they can try for her. Thank you that the next step seems so obvious. Thank you for her good attitude so far, for the way she is always in the present moment. I learn so much from her.

Of course, You know my heart and I am anxious and fearful about the surgery itself. Help me deal with those feelings, and do not let them overwhelm me. Help me to focus on the present as Aggie does, to put my heart into doing what is in front of me. May my doing be Your doing, that she truly may be served in love.

Once it was decided that Aggie would have surgery, we wanted it done as soon as possible. Everything came together to make that happen: she was discharged on Thursday, and we were to return the following Tuesday for pre-surgery appointments and surgery on Wednesday.

We had a long weekend in front of us, and decided to spend it with our families in Michigan. My stomach was in knots all weekend, not only dreading the surgery but also observing how the rest of the family shared our struggles. Were we gathered to say good-bye to sick Aggie, only to welcome healthy Aggie back into our lives again? Or were we saying a longer goodbye?

Aggie knew little of her family's emotional struggles. She heard us talking about surgery, but in her special way seemed to care nothing about it. She jumped on every scooter ride offered, and, when she was not too tired, she joined in all of the family wrestling matches. More often, we would notice her staring off into space, looking tired and sick. Yet she gladly received every hug and snuggle from everyone around, not caring that they had tears in their eyes while they gave her their love.

Lord, I know how much it hurts to love Aggie while she goes through this awful thing. Thank you so much for all the other people who, despite the hurt, allow her into their hearts. You truly have surrounded this suffering child with love. She is slipping away, becoming unaware of more and more things...Lord, make a way through the fog for at least this one thing: Help her always to be aware of how very much she is loved.

Though there were many things she no longer was able to do, Aggie retained this important skill: she was weak, but she was loved. She did not try to hide her weaknesses as an adult would, as her mommy did, but she bore them out in the open and allowed everyone else to experience her trials with her. She had an amazing ability to passively receive love and grace. That was not something I ever thought was a "skill," yet I began to see that it is. Afflicted and suffering, Aggie lived with open hands and an open heart, willingly and gratefully receiving every drop of love and help offered to her.

Sharing her burden, we could not help but shower her with love and affection, even though the only kind we had to offer was tainted with grief, pain, and weariness. Through the fog, her Heavenly Father's love poured down on her through us, through the medical team that cared for her, through everyone that knew her and loved her. It was raining, even pouring, and this small withering flower received every drop and soaked it in. We watched, and waited, not knowing whether our tiny flower was going to bloom again in this life; or whether the flood would overwhelm her, wash her away from us, and whisk her into her Father's arms.

Chapter 30
The Night Before Surgery

July 14, 2009

It was the evening before surgery. I knew the next day would be one of those days by which we mark time. July 14 would be our last day "before Aggie's brain surgery," and everything that was to come would be known as time "after Aggie's brain surgery." How should we spend one last night "before surgery" with our sick little Aggie?

We took Aggie on a walk to Lake Erie in the afternoon. We let her run around in the grass and the sunshine. I chased her and gave her a good *(last?)* wrestling match. Later in the hotel room, we had a feast with fried chicken and chocolate milk and a ridiculous amount of candy. Friends came to see her, grandparents, and big sister Lorraine. They all got to squeeze in a few *(last?)* tickles and snuggles and hugs. I took lots of video, just in case. I joined the others in trying to infuse that one evening with all the life and fun that we could.

I couldn't help but notice that Aggie did not feel the weight of those moments as we did. She had no desire to soak up each little experience, to store them away somewhere just in case things never returned to normal. She did not breathe in the fresh air deeply enough, she did not enjoy her last evening with hair as I would if I were her. She was just being a kid; bouncing from one thing to the next, fluttering around as if this were just another day, taking those everyday blessings—the sunshine, the wind in her hair, the running and playing—for granted.

Finally, we turned out the lights, and she went right to sleep. I lay in bed with my eyes open, wishing I was more like Aggie. *She knows what is coming tomorrow, yet she sleeps soundly. And why should she worry? God who gave her joy in the sunshine today will hold her close in the valley tomorrow.*

Deliver her from evil, Lord, I prayed earnestly. Those were the words I used at least, words I had been taught, and words that, on the surface, seemed to express this mother's desire for health for her suffering child. But did I mean them? I wanted Aggie healthy and better, and wasn't my entire life at this pointed dedicated to that most worthy end? Hadn't I proven that I would spare no expense and go to any extreme if it would make my baby better?

Health and life are good things, obviously, gifts from God. But are they always what is *best?* Not at all, and the more I prayed to my Heavenly Father, the more I was gently reminded that I did not know what was truly best for Aggie. I knew what I wanted, I knew what seemed good, but I did not really know what was best. If more words were added to my prayers so that they truly exposed my heart, they would sound something like this:

Deliver her from evil, Lord, especially the kind of evil that causes me pain, too. Keep her here with me, and make her healthy and whole. Having her here in this world of sin and suffering seems so much better than saying goodbye. It is better for me. If You called her home to be with You…well, I guess she would truly be delivered from all evil, but God help me, I don't think I would be able to bear it. Deliver ME from evil, Lord, by which I mean my own suffering.

Keep seizures and sickness away, restore Aggie to health, and give me a lifetime to love and enjoy her. That's all I ask.

I never directly laid those words in front of God, but every time I prayed I struggled with those feelings. I was intensely aware of my own selfishness in my prayers. I was on my knees, trembling with the knowledge that God had control of the situation and that I had none at all. I knew that things may not go my way; that I might even be forced to admit that the ultimate good of my dear child called for the most unimaginable pain on my part. I knew my heart clung to her too tightly. I knew my white-knuckled grip on her life would be no match for God if He chose to take her away. And I knew He had every right to do so.

This was the deep fear that haunted me, even more than the nasty images of the surgery itself. Not even for a moment was I able to purge the sin and selfishness from my heart, to truly lay her in God's hands and sincerely pray for His will to be done. The fire of this trial exposed me again and again for what I am: a mess of sin and selfishness, with no right to come before God with a list of demands.

I was tempted to simply grit my teeth, hold my breath, close my eyes and wait for the storm to pass, in hopes that at least my adrenaline would keep my body moving. But I was too weak to even do that. I gave up the vain attempts to hide these ugly things from God, and came to Him the only way I could: as a beggar. Weary, weak, and sinful, I brought all of this mess to the throne of God. Through the rest of the waiting, the preparations, and even in my sleep, my heart lay exposed before God, repeating one simple petition:

I know she's Yours, Lord; but please don't take her.

Chapter 31
Mind Games

July 15, 2009

The morning of her surgery, Aggie woke up wiggly and wild, as usual. She played with Eldon, got herself dressed, and goofed around, not wondering why her parents were so heavy-hearted. We sat together on the hotel bed so we could pray together before we left for the hospital. This unusual event, combined with her daddy's tears, turned her carefree fluttering into wide-eyed seriousness.

The morning of the surgery I was glad for the liturgy. Neither Josh nor I had the ability to pull spiritual thoughts or feelings out of our own hearts; we could only come to God with our need. Yet His Word and the words of the liturgy spoke to us and for us. "*I believe in God, the Father Almighty, maker of heaven and earth. And in Jesus Christ, His only Son, our Lord.*"[7] We sang and spoke those familiar and comforting words, solid words, words that reminded us of God our Rock, of eternal truth that is so much bigger than these momentary afflictions.

> *Glory be to the Father and to the Son,*
> *and to the Holy Ghost.*
> *As it was in the beginning, is now,*
> *and ever shall be, world without end.*
> *Amen.*[8]

I took Aggie's hand in mine and set my face for the hospital. I still did not know how the King would rule, but I knew He was good.

As we waited for the medical staff, Aggie sat in the hospital bed holding her new Dr. Bear. He in his scrubs and she in her gown, they cheerfully waited to be taken to surgery. The doctor listened to Aggie's heart, and Dr. Bear's heart, and assured her that they were both ready for surgery. The nurse gave her some "pre-medicine" to make the sedation process easier on her. It made the waiting process a bit easier on her parents as well, as she entertained us with all kinds of hilarious stories and songs while she waited. She sang us a slow, slurred version of "Zip-a-Dee-Doo-Dah" and her ABCs, roughly in the right order. She poured out her heart to us as if she were inebriated. "I loooooove you Daddy! You are the best, Daddy! And I looooooove Mommy! And that little Eldie Eldie—he's a cutie baby, cutie baby, cutie baby, cute! And I love my buddies! And I love you Mommy...."

Finally, they took our smiling child to that room where the real work would begin. I could have counted that moment as my workout for the day: the wrestling I did inside myself in order to let her go. There was a part of me that wanted to grab the gurney, pull her away from those people with needles and drills, and keep her safe with me. *No you may not do those awful things to my baby!* But she was not safe with me either, and so I let her go.

I held my breath from that point on, but somehow my body kept moving. Family and friends provided helpful distractions, and their very presence gave me a reason not to curl up in a ball and cry until it was all over. It was such an awful thing to contemplate, allowing people to drill into my child's brain, and to wonder whether it may be just one more unsuccessful attempt to help her; so I tried not to contemplate anything.

I wanted to know as little as possible about the actual details of the surgery. I would be curious if it was somebody else, or something on a television show; but I did not think I could bear the ugly, bloody truths when spoken about my own daughter. I wanted to be wholly ignorant of titanium plates, peeling back scalps, drilling into bone, and all of the awful details. For once I did not Google, I looked at no pictures, I sought no details. Despite all of these efforts, images assaulted me during the surgery. I may have appeared to be reading with my oldest daughter, or taking a peaceful walk around the city while we waited, but in my mind, I was doing mental martial arts.

Whatever I saw in front of me might suddenly be blocked out by an awful image of my baby's head in a giant clamp. Instinctively I would let fly a mental roundhouse kick, expelling the image and grabbing on quickly to whatever distraction was directly in front of me. *Thank you God for this bagel and coffee.* My mind might throw in a grating drill sound, but a quick mental uppercut would knock that nasty noise out of the universe so that I could get back to coloring with Lorraine. If blue-lipped Aggie, motionless on a bleak hospital bed, should haunt my peripheral vision, a hearty mental jab would send her away, and a snuggly baby Eldon would remind his mother of life and health.

These inner aerobics went on for hours that felt like days and months, until, finally, we were notified that her surgery was over. "She did great, no complications, and we got all of the tumor." I began to breathe again, just a little, as I raced to see her, yearning to hold my living, breathing baby in my arms once again.

I had expected, assuming the surgery went well, to feel nothing but relief and joy when it was finally over. I did not expect new arrows to pierce my heart. I was ready to take a break from the martial arts, but it was not yet time. As is standard after brain surgery, Aggie was placed in the ICU for the first night. She was propped up in bed, head bandaged, monitors, wires and tubes attached all over her body. It was not the sight of Aggie that upset me. I had expected her to look like she had just had major surgery. It was the sound.

Aggie was crying, and it was an awful cry. Her eyes were hardly open, but she moaned, whined, reached, and squirmed. She seemed intent on something, yet so terribly confused. We could not figure out what she wanted. She was utterly miserable. She did not respond to my presence, nor to anyone else's. She cried, moaned, reached and squirmed, babbling constantly, and she could not be comforted.

How I hate those awful problems that cannot be touched with mommy love! The nurses and doctors seemed unsettled by her behavior as well, but explained that she was "probably having a bad reaction to the anesthesia." *Probably?* So that I could survive, my mind grabbed on to that explanation, and I resumed mental aerobics to keep away other possibilities. Josh and I, the grandparents, and friends took turns trying to comfort her throughout the evening.

Whatever was bothering her seemed to stop for brief periods. She spoke a little, enough to convince us that she knew we were there. Then, the crying and insisting on whatever-it-was would resume, and we did not know how to help her. She slipped in and out of sleep, waking each time with tears and babbling. When she was not sleeping, she continued moaning, hallucinating, and writhing in her bed, inconsolable.

Machines beeped, nurses rushed in and out, and Aggie moaned. I stood at her bedside, touching her warm skin, trying in vain to comfort her and myself. We made it through surgery, and they said it was successful. *So where was my relief?*

Josh was to stay in the hospital that night, so I returned to the Ronald MacDonald House with Josh's parents, Eldon, and Lorraine. Their presence was a comfort and an incentive to keep myself together for a little bit longer. When we got back to the room, I put the kids to bed and got in the shower. The hot water and the solitude were welcome, as the images of the day washed over me. I tried to focus on the reported "success" of the surgery, and to block out the sound of Aggie's incoherent groaning that was still ringing in my ears. As I reached for the shampoo, I slipped. When I hit the floor of the bathtub, pain shot through my back, and somehow the pain completely destroyed every one of my coping mechanisms. All the thoughts I had been trying to keep away suddenly overcame me. *What have we done? She's been ruined, and we let them do it!* Her awful noises rang in my ears over and over while I cried. *Is she even "in there" anymore? What have we done?* I had no energy left for mental aerobics. Drained of all strength and willpower, I simply let the fears attack and the tears fall.

I managed to get myself together and to bed, but it was a long time before I slept.

God will not forsake us...but if He did, would it look much different?

Chapter 32
Spunk

July 16, 2009

The next morning I awoke to the phone ringing. It was Aggie. "Hi, Mommy," Aggie said quietly. I jumped out of bed, smiling. She still sounded like she was in pain, but she was talking! She was rational! She was Aggie! I could not move quickly enough to get myself back to the hospital and get that girl in my arms. She really did make it through surgery!

When I got to the hospital, I found an ornery but much-improved little girl. She was still connected to all kinds of tubes and wires, and she was quite upset that the IV on her hand made it impossible to play the "cake game" on the computer. She had not eaten anything in two days, per doctors orders, and would not be allowed to do so until they got her in for her post-surgery MRI. Due to her tubes and wires, she was not allowed out of her bed even to use the bathroom, and she was horribly offended when offered a diaper.

"You can leave now," said a scowling Aggie to the man who saved her life that morning. I doubt that this esteemed neuro-surgeon is often dismissed in this way by his patients, but Aggie was no respecter of persons. She scowled through her various checkups and labs. She tried to think of ways to make herself happy, but was thwarted at every turn.

"Can I have some chocolate milk?"

"No, Honey, nothing until after your MRI."

"Can I go potty?"

"No, Honey, you can't get out of bed. Can I help you do it there?"

"No! Can I play the cake game?"

"No, Aggie, you have to leave the IV port in your hand until after the MRI."

"Can we go home?"

"No, Honey, I'm sorry!"

Aggie was sick of her bed, sick of her IVs and wires, sick of her room, sick of feeling sick. She did not hesitate to let everyone around her know that she was *not pleased.* She even took a swing at me once, followed quickly by an "I'm sorry, Mama!" and a hearty meltdown.

Though it was hard to see her so miserable, it was a huge relief to see her in her right mind. I was thankful for even her grumpy attitude, and called it "spunk." Her eyes were glassy from all the medicines they had given her, constantly making us question whether she was about to have a seizure. I was always bracing for that, knowing that no matter what I told myself beforehand, seeing even one seizure after surgery would be devastating.

She had no seizures, but also no food and no MRI for several hours that day. Mixed with her intense hunger were steroids (for inflammation) and side effects from the anesthesia. Aggie was pushed to her limits that afternoon. She decided she wanted mommy snuggles, so I crawled into bed with her. She had strong opinions about exactly where I put my head, where I put each hand, and she demanded that I keep my eyes closed, too. She finally fell asleep, just minutes before they came to get her for her MRI. To protect a few more minutes of her precious sleep, I rode right in bed with her down to radiology.

When she woke up she found a new group of medical people invading a new room, and she tried in vain to order them all out. "Can I play the cake game? Can I please?"

she begged me, over and over and over, crying and refusing to take "no" for an answer. They finally gave her some medicine to calm her, and after a few minutes she began to settle down. Even sleep did not totally overtake her determination. As she drifted off, she crossed her arms and said, "FINE, Mommy, I will just never, never, never do the cake game again." She fell asleep, but every few minutes she stirred and muttered, "never, never, never again."

After the MRI we returned to ICU for more observation and waiting. Lorraine crawled into bed with Aggie and they watched Tom and Jerry. Aggie finally got to eat and drink a little bit, and the scowl creases on her face relaxed ever so slightly. It was a comfort for Aggie to have Lorraine there, and the nurses welcomed and included Big Sister whenever they could. They allowed the girls to ride together when Aggie was transported to the pediatric floor, and they even let Lorraine help reapply the leads for Aggie's heart and lung monitors.

We moved to the pediatric floor into a large, private room with more space, fewer wires, and slightly less noise. Aggie was exhausted and ready for bed by about seven, but again, her plan was thwarted. The new nurses had to check her vitals once more, get her reattached to all of the monitors, and so on. It seemed like they always needed to do one last thing. She sat and scowled. I decided to leave around 9:30 p.m., but Aggie insisted I never, ever leave.

"Aggie, I know you wanted to do crafts today. I need to leave so I can go back to the room and get a craft for us to do tomorrow."

"No, Mommy, I don't want you to go," she whined, and crossed her arms. "You'll just have to do a craft *all* by *yourself* tomorrow." She looked away from me. I kissed her scowling forehead, and tried not to let her see my little smile as I left.

Josh turned down the lights and began to prepare for the night. Just as our feisty little girl looked like she would finally be settling down for sleep, she caught him off guard. She sat straight up in bed and ripped the IV port right out of her ankle. The events that followed will probably be known by the nurses and all the patients on that floor as *The Great IV War of 2009*. Our sweet four-year-old little lady, who happened to be grumpy and on steroids, put up an amazing fight. After wrestling and tears and bruises all around, the best efforts of the "IV swat team" finally succeeded. Josh called me on the phone around eleven, hoping my voice would soothe her out of hysterics. It eventually did, and she slept soundly for the rest of the night.

July 17, 2009

Every day after the surgery, Aggie seemed to get a little bit better. Friday was her first day without a single painful medical procedure, and she was much more cheerful. Her grandparents were able to get quite a few laughs out of her that day. She and Lorraine enjoyed a delicious gummy-worm and water tea party right there in her hospital bed. They ended up spilling, then slurping up the spilled water from the plates like dogs, and laughing hysterically. Yes, life was getting a little bit closer to normal again.

As I snuggled Aggie in her hospital bed that afternoon, I thought of another hospital bed several years ago, the one where I curled up with little newborn Aggie and spent the day praising God for the miracle of life.

There was some pain mixed with joy on the day Aggie was born. My labor with her still holds the record for my worst ever. My body ached from those eleven hours of hor-rific back labor with no drugs, and my heart ached for my husband who was serving in Iraq instead of snuggling her with me.

When Aggie was born, the medical world that she was born into seemed almost irrelevant. My midwife caught her and cleaned her up, but that was about it. The credit went to God who made her, and who made my body that grew and delivered her. And when it was over, I felt like we had just gone through the hardest thing ever, my little one and I...Yet there, in that recovery bed, there was nothing but the sweet smell of newborn skin, soft snuggles, relief, and the sleep of happy exhaustion.

In our new hospital bed, we also had exhaustion, joy, and relief, but that is not all. The pains of brain surgery and everything that preceded it were far greater than a mere eleven hours of labor. And so, the recovery would take lon-ger, for my little one and for her mother.

The world of medical professionals was not irrelevant that time. We laid there, one small family in an enormous hospital. We had to be careful how we moved in that recov-ery bed because there were tubes and wires everywhere that helped her care team monitor her heart, lungs, blood pres-sure, oxygen level; that kept her hydrated and medicated as needed; that slowly filled a deflated child with life and health.

One hundred years ago, Aggie's story would have been much different. The technology that pinpointed the prob-lem and made it possible to remove her tumor simply was not there. Back then, we would have had very little hope for her future. We would have watched, helplessly, as she got progressively worse, until she finally died.

Snuggling Aggie in that recovery bed, I did not feel responsible at all for the miracle that took place. I praised

God, not for the way my body works, but for the way that hospital works, for the medical professionals of all kinds who devote their lives to research and healing. I praised God for the gifts and skills He gave to them, and for their willingness to use them to serve others. I praised God for people who can handle giving screaming children IVs, emptying bedpans, and drilling into skulls, so that my baby can have a future.

"Now there are varieties of gifts, but the same Spirit; and there are varieties of service, but the same Lord; and there are varieties of activities, but it is the same God who empowers them all in everyone." (1 Corinthians 12:4-6)

Chapter 33

Bruises

Aggie was discharged from the hospital on Saturday, a mere three days after brain surgery. Her discharge papers said, "Activity restrictions: none." I immediately questioned the nurse, "Are you serious? She can really go on the playground, ride a bike, whatever?"

"She sure can!" the nurse replied. "Just don't let her rub mud on her wound!" So, we were told to keep her from rolling in mud, and out of the water for six weeks; but other than that, she was given permission to be a normal kid again.

The second she was free of her wires and tubes, she was off to the play room. She was hopping, skipping, even running! I kept saying things like, "Slow down, kiddo! Don't you realize you just had brain surgery?" She was able to keep her hair, but the five-inch long wound on her head was still quite obvious. It made me cringe every time I saw it, especially if she was running or climbing.

Aggie looked like she had been through a war after surgery. She had battle wounds of all kinds: bruises on her head from the clamp that held her still during surgery; bruises from the blood draws and IV attempts; and mysterious bruises, likely from one of her many wrestling matches with the staff. We never did count them because she refused to sit still long enough, but I am sure she had at least thirty. We called them "polka dots," and they did not seem to bother her at all.

We were welcomed back home by happy and relieved family members and friends. Our home was filled with gifts, cards, balloons, food; gifts of joy that reminded us how many people had shared this experience with us. And all the while, healthy, smiling Aggie fluttered around like a hummingbird and danced in the sunshine.

Despite all the blessings around me, when we returned home, my heart was dull, almost numb. Now and then a little joy and thanksgiving would bubble up, but strangely, it was rare. We had been through a nasty, violent storm. I imagined our immediate family out in a boat, weathering the worst of it. On the shore, our friends and family had been watching, waiting, praying with us and for us. They had shared our fears and the dark nights, and they probably often felt helpless as they watched the storm toss us all over the place, striking blow after blow after blow. Yet they remained steadfast in prayer for us, and loved us through it.

After surgery, the storm had died down. The land was green, freshly watered, and bursting with life and health. Our family's boat made it safely back to shore, and those who shared our burden were throwing a party. They were rejoicing, praising the Lord, and celebrating His amazing deliverance.

I still was weary from those days at sea. I was out of breath, shaken, bruised, and battered. I got off the boat and collapsed on the sand, faintly praising God, yet still afraid. *Did I just hear thunder in the distance? Was it the sound of that awful storm leaving, or is another going to strike before we recover?*

Aggie came home with bruises and wounds, and I think her mommy did, too. That knot I carried in my chest during her surgery did not simply go away when it was all over. My body was still weary, and my heart was full of reservations. I was still bracing for another seizure, for that one awful moment that would send us right back into misery. Mere days of seizure freedom would not make that worry go away. Yes, she seemed healthy now, but I saw vividly that all of this health and happiness was so horribly fragile. It might be shattered at any minute.

My eyes had been opened to a reality that made me very uncomfortable. Even if my little Aggie was better, the world was still fragile, everyone I loved was fragile and mortal, and part of me still hated that. Two hundred seizure-free days would not give me the security in this world that I so wanted.

I felt in my heart a potential for a secret grudge about the whole situation; a subtle, yet powerful, feeling towards God that He had wronged us in some way. *Why did my baby have to go through that in the first place, God? Even if she is better, which I can't even really count on...it was just so, so horrible!* He was still my loving Father, still my Refuge Who had brought me through this awful thing. Yet because of this awful thing, I had become powerfully aware that I did not, could not always understand Him or His ways. **"'For My thoughts are not your thoughts, neither are your ways my ways,' declares the Lord. 'As the heavens are higher than the earth, so are my ways higher than your ways, and my thoughts than your thoughts.'" (Isaiah 55:8-9)** This is God's Word—Truth—but sometimes it is a very hard truth to bear. My withering flower was blooming once again, but my own wounds still hurt, and they would take some time to heal.

Again, my Father did not forsake me to these feelings, nor did He allow my unanswered questions to keep me from His steadfast love. Gently, He turned my eyes to Himself, reminding me that only in His eternal care will I find that security that I so long for. In this life and in the next, He is the only Solid thing. Though I am selfish, He has mercy. Though I question and fight Him, He is faithful. Though I am weak, He loves.

⊱✦⊰

He had no obligation to do so, yet God graciously showered on us day after day of seizure freedom. He gave us an Aggie in bloom once again. He restored her energy, and her joy for life. The door to my heart creaked open ever so slowly, and He gave me the courage to love healthy Aggie again.

I remember the moment the dam burst. It was about a week after surgery. Aggie and the other children were eating lunch; jabbering, teasing, joking around the table. I wish I could remember the joke that inspired The Laugh that broke down all of my walls, but I cannot. I only carry the memory of an unexpected moment, a sudden, shocking lightning bolt of joy that went from her lips to my heart.

It was a girly little giggle, a giggle that turned into a beautiful and contagious belly laugh. It took me completely by surprise. I had forgotten she could laugh like that. She used to do it all the time, but I had forgotten. I had been loving sick Aggie for so long that I had forgotten many things about the way she used to be. *The way she is again.*

July 22, 2009
Lord, what a storm we have been through. Might it be over, really? Aggie is now on day seven of seizure freedom. I hardly can believe my eyes, hardly dare to let myself hope this could be for good. At least, that is how I felt until I heard that laugh last night. Oh, Lord, I had forgotten she could laugh like that! It was like music, like pure joy, an echo of angelic bliss right from the heavens. I had forgotten...so much about her sweet spirit. It is as if the Aggie we

used to know has been raised from the dead! Oh, Jesus, dare I let myself love her this way? It is too great, too much risk, too wonderful to believe! That laugh...it seemed to shatter all the restraints I had put on my hope and joy—I can hardly stop these tears of gratitude!

Oh, Jesus, how you have carried us. There were times when I felt so alone and desperate, as if you had forsaken us. My heart was so overwhelmed with trial and suffering I could see nothing else. There is still a bruise, Lord. You know my heart. There is still some pain and that awful question: Why do You make some flowers bloom and allow others to wither?

Yet my flower is blooming, and dancing, and flourishing after a long sickness. I can't help but rejoice, and the joy is pushing those unanswered questions far back in my mind...until the next trial. I do not fully understand You, Lord, but I know enough today to praise and thank You with my whole heart!

Chapter 34
Reasons to Pray

September, 2009

Healthy Aggie is a beautiful thing. Her laugh returned, and her smile once again reached her eyes. The knot in my stomach began to melt. I rejoiced, and I wondered: *Is normal Aggie really back again? And is she back to stay? And was she this beautiful before she got sick?*

Because she has weathered such a trial, Aggie is tougher than the others when it comes to minor injuries. She crashed on her scooter that fall, and even though her eye was almost swollen shut with the injury, she jumped right back on. As her brain healed from the surgery, she continued to take anti-epilepsy medicines for several months. Each month she had to get a blood draw to monitor the drug levels. The last time I took her, I was completely amazed at her bravery. What was once an occasion for screaming and wrestling, she faced with quiet resolve, and the courage of Peter Pan.

Unlike her big sister, Aggie hates having her hair brushed. Lorraine cheerfully sits with me while I brush and braid and play. She likes her hair to be smooth and shiny, and takes time to do her hair even if I forget. Aggie hates every second of it. When I call her into the bathroom and she sees me holding the brush, she protests, "Mommy, but I have to make my bed!" or, "Hurry up, Mommy, so I don't miss Super Why!" As I brush, she inches towards the door, and wiggles impatiently as if that will help the process go more quickly. Sometimes she moans and whines as if I am torturing her. I remember one time, weeks after her surgery, she yelled, "*Mommy, you are brushing on my owie!!!*" She cried and held her head with a pathetic look on her face.

"Honey," I said, "Your owie is on the other side."

"Oh." She said, suppressing a smile. I smiled and shook my head. *All right, I will hurry up so you can get back to your every day party.*

⚜

Aggie no longer had seizures, but she was not exactly normal. Little quirks remained. The quirks were hard to define, hard to explain. Each odd behavior made me question: Is this from the surgery? Is it the medicine she is still on? Is this just something unique about her? Does it mean she's getting sick again?

The most noticeable quirk was that she had trouble finding words. Conversation with her remained difficult, as she could think much more quickly than she could communicate.

One day I let her take a nap in my room. After about an hour (not near enough time for a typical Aggie-sized nap,) Aggie came out of my room. "Mommy, I'm ready to get up now. I sleep-ded already." I knew this was untrue, because she looked relatively put together for Aggie. When she really does sleep, she comes out of her room looking like she's just had a ride on a helicopter.

"Aggie, did you really sleep?"

Her mouth was going a million miles a minute already. "Oh, yes, Mommy, I sleep-ded really good. I sleep-ded in your bed and I am ready to get up now. But, Mommy…I have to show you something." She got very serious and took my hand. I let her lead me into my room to the table by the side of my bed. My digital clock said 11:37pm.

"Mommy, I sleep-ded but the numbers...the numbers...I don't know what happened to the numbers because I sleep-ded really good and my feet were under the covers and...I was being good...and my feet were sleeping under the covers...and, look, I made your bed for you...and I'm really sorry, Mommy...but my feet where under the covers but the numbers...I don't...my feet...I sleep-ded I really did...my feet were being good...." A pause, then finally, a confession, "....maybe my fingers did it."

Patience and creativity were required to make sense of much of Aggie's speech. I wondered whether this would improve with time, whether she would be able to keep up with her peers when she finally started kindergarten. I spoke with her neurologist about it. He said the medicine may or may not be to blame. We would only know for sure once she was weaned off it, a process which we would wait months to begin. He also reminded me that her year of seizures basically had take away a year of development and learning. Though she was now five years old, I ought not be surprised to see behaviors that are typical of a younger child.

Those words encouraged me when I observed her strangest behaviors. Some days it seemed like she turned back into sick Aggie (minus the seizures), even just for hours at a time. She would put things in her mouth like a baby, or try to chew on strange things like the monkey bars. I found her talking to herself, muttering, and even trying to isolate herself from the other children. (That would have been unheard of before seizures.) She absolutely never could miss a nap or she became completely goofy—uncoordinated, confused; even doing odd, repetitive things. But these things were blips, mere days or even hours, that invaded long stretches of what seemed to be normal Aggie behavior.

As I became comfortable with the more normal version of Aggie, when I did notice quirks I became frustrated and worried. Even though she seemed better, I tried to make myself remember all she had been through. Though I wanted to declare her cured in my mind and rush back to loving healthy Aggie, I could not do that. I learned to cut her a little slack, and accept the fact that she still had special needs. If I could look at her that way, then her quirks were just quirks, and they become much easier for me to handle. I told myself that her special needs may go away after she was off the meds and completely healed from surgery; but for now they are here, undefined, and unpredictable. My prayer each day remained, *Lord, help me to love THIS Aggie.* Her quirks kept me praying for her, and her example often taught me how to pray for others.

I remember one day, I held Seth and tried to comfort him while Daddy removed a sliver from his finger. His screams did seem to me to be warranted by the situation. I murmured small words of comfort while I inwardly rolled my eyes. I rarely panic when I hear a child scream for me now. Slivers and stings are part of life, and, of course, "Sweetie, I am sorry that it hurts, but it could be so, so much worse. Come child, sit here, and mommy will fix it." A bandage, a hug, and a good book will lessen the smart of these little wounds. It is only a sliver; hardly brain surgery!

As I stroked Seth's hair, I saw Aggie looking at us with worried eyes. "It's okay, Honey, Seth just has a sliver."

She nodded, sat down right where she was and prayed, "Jesus, please help Seth's toe to get feeling better quick and help him to be brave. Amen."

It does not occur to this child to compare the trials of others with her own. If someone is hurt, she prays. If someone is sad, she prays. If someone is sick, she prays. Any and all trials are worthy of her compassion, important enough for her to take into her hands and bring into the presence of God. She knows her Father, our Father, will help. She continues to humble me, even in health.

Chapter 35
Sun on the Road

October, 2009

We had been sitting in the van for hours, and I sensed a restlessness that would get ugly if I did not intervene. It would be at least two more hours until we reached Grandma's house. Naps were completed, snacks dispersed, and the activity bag was empty. Fidgety bodies began invading the spaces of other bodies, and the complaining voices were reaching a higher pitch. My husband's jaw tensed as he turned up the radio, keeping his eyes on the road. Yes, quiet mommy-time was over, too quickly as always. I set down my book and climbed in the back with the children. It was time to entertain. "Okay, children, I'm thinking of a fun place. Ask me yes-or-no questions for clues."

"I want to think of the place this time!"

"No! I want to!"

"Kids! If you want to play, then I will be the one picking the place, and you all will be the guessers. That's it. Now, if you want to play and you have a yes-or-no question for me, please raise your hand. Yes, Lorraine."

"Is it in Indiana?"

"No, it is not in Indiana." Thinking of Grandma's house, the very place we were heading, I smiled. I was trying to make this first one easy to guess.

"Is it Dairy Queen?"

"No, Seth, and remember to raise your hand next time. Yes, Aggie, what is your question?"

"Mommy, is it that fun place with the green popsicles? You know, and the train place and the movies?"

"Oh, Honey, do you mean Cleveland Clinic?" I laughed. Aggie really considers Cleveland Clinic a fun place! "No, I wasn't thinking of Cleveland Clinic. You think the hospital is a pretty fun place?"

"Yes, Mommy!" she insisted. "I had a tea party with Lorraine and I ate ice cream," she smiled as the memories came flooding back, "and we watched Tom and Jerry, and I had to have surgery and I didn't like to have surgery," she scowled slightly, but then remembered, "AND I got to bring Curious George, you and me played in that park with the flowers, and then we went to the hotel and we went swimming! Can we go there again, Mommy? Please?"

I smiled. Our post-surgery game of hide and seek in the "park" (the garden at the Ronald MacDonald house) will forever be one of my favorite memories. It was too hot for outdoor games, really, but there was so much joy and relief in the air we simply could not help it. It was the day she was discharged from the hospital. I held Eldon on my hip while the girls ran around, through flowers and over bridges. Lorraine was excited to run free with her sister, and was probably also grateful to see the adults around her finally stop acting so serious! Aggie was bursting with energy, so happy to be freed from her IVs and wires, so ready to be out of that hospital bed.

They disappeared, giggled, and I pretended to have trouble finding them. They jumped out of bushes to "scare" me, and Eldon laughed as I feigned fear. Aggie left my sight, healthy, and then she came back, still healthy. It surprised and delighted me every time.

"Yes, Honey, you will be going to Cleveland Clinic again pretty soon. But you won't have to have surgery this time." Three months after surgery, and Aggie was still seizure-free. All evidence seemed to prove the theory that the tumor was the problem. No tumor, no seizures. Days of ceaseless Aggie-talking piled upon one another, and once again we could imagine life uninterrupted by seizures.

We imagined, but we did not take her days of health for granted. Her tumor was not a WHO Grade I DNET (dysembryoplastic neuroepithelial tumor), as the doctors suspected. The pathology report classified her tumor as an oligoastrocytoma, a Grade II brain tumor. The tumor was not yet malignant, and if the surgeon got the entire tumor, every single cell, it will not come back. If it does come back, it likely will return as a more aggressive Grade III or Grade IV tumor. She will require surgery again, if surgery is possible, along with chemotherapy and radiation. The cause of the tumor is completely unknown. It is extremely rare to see this kind of tumor in a child. Her long term prognosis is uncertain.

Aggie will need frequent MRIs for the next ten years. Should that time pass with no changes, the doctors will declare her cured. *Ten years.* That is a long time to stare at her head and wonder. Ten years is a long time to try to love her without becoming too attached to her; to hold her with an open hand and tense muscles, bracing for that moment when she slips away again.

Do I dare let her in? Can I allow myself to love healthy Aggie again, knowing how vulnerable that makes me? If I spend my time mentally rehearsing, will I face the day of trial with a smile and calm submission this time? Considering my heart, the answer obviously is no. The only way I could maintain that kind of "strength" would be if I closed my heart to her completely. Of course, if I constantly try to protect myself from anxiety and pain, at the end of the day, I will not have loved her.

I looked at my healthy daughter sitting next to me in the van, full of happy memories about Cleveland Clinic. She held her Curious George doll and insisted we get back to the game.

"Mommy, is it the jungle? The jungle is a fun place!"

She had never been to the jungle, of course, but Curious George seems to have plenty of fun there in the movie. I could imagine Aggie swinging through the trees with a monkey, laughing like she does as she swings across the monkey bars now. Add that to the long list of new skills she had acquired since her surgery, now that she was able to learn things again.

"Aggie the jungle is NOT fun. There are HUGE spiders there, and tigers too," corrected Lorraine.

"If I saw a spider or a tiger, I'd just fly away from them like Peter Pan," Aggie quipped. She tried to keep her face serious, but her eyes danced as she teased. I smiled as the banter continued.

God help me, I cannot help but love her. God help me, I love her too much. I love all of them too much. If I could possess them and hide them away, put them on a shelf and delight in them forever, I would do it. My "love" is tainted, seeking my own good in and with theirs. The truth is, I just do not know what truly is best for them. My eyes and my love are clouded. I know what I want and what I fear, but I do not always know what is good. Only God does, and that scares me.

Days of trial will return, but I have not been told when or of what kind. I do know this: Worry stops nothing. Mental rehearsals do nothing. I cannot prepare my own heart for that day in a hypothetical world. God never asked me to do that. He sees the sin that mixes itself with my love. Yet He has mercy, in Jesus, giving daily forgiveness and strength for the daily demands of love. He gives daily bread; He strengthens me in days of health and sickness.

Should Aggie return to weakness, I will return to weakness with her. My resources will fail me instantly, but God will be there to supply what is lacking. Today, her body is strong. It is strong by the grace of God, and for no other reason. He who sustains her body and mine, who sustained our faith through the days of darkness, will uphold us again when darkness comes.

Father, the sun is warm and constant today, and it soothes and heals me. I can almost forget how forsaken I felt in the winter. An argument lingers for a moment...wait, Lord, I want an explanation, not just relief! The bruise on my heart remains, but the ice that formed over it is melting away under Your kindness. I am silenced by the warmth of the sun. Here in this place of beauty it is hard to remember what I was complaining about so loudly.

What can I do but soak up the sun on the days it is given to me? The weather will change again, but Your faithfulness is constant. Today, the sun is out and I am healing.

"Your steadfast love, O LORD, extends to the heavens, Your faithfulness to the clouds."
(Psalm 36:5)

Epilogue

August 16, 2010

Today is Aggie's 397th day of seizure-freedom, and her first day of kindergarten. She recovered from brain surgery as if it were merely a haircut. Because her tumor was extremely rare, she continues to need MRIs every three months. The shadow lingers, but uncertainty does not block the light of the sun. Its warm, healing light shines on Aggie, and each day without seizures is adorned with other tiny miracles of growth.

At 6:30 this morning, Aggie bounced out of bed, ripped off her pajamas, and threw on her "beautiful new dress" to wear to kindergarten. While Lorraine was still rubbing sleep out of her eyes, Aggie put on some "dancing music" and cheerfully made her sister's bed and her own. Her singing woke the boys before I had my first sip of coffee. I sighed, then smiled.

To Aggie, on your first day of kindergarten,

Today, my Aggie flower is dancing off to school, ready to bloom in another garden. You and Lorraine have been chattering excitedly about school for weeks now. When we went school shopping last week, the only thing you insisted that you have was a green backpack, because green makes you think of Peter Pan. You wore your beloved green backpack throughout our shopping trip, and tenderly buckled it in the seat next to you for the ride home! Now it bounces along on your back as you skip off to your first day of school. My brave girl is facing her next milestone with wide open arms, a light heart, and that huge Aggie smile I love so much.

As you leave your pre-school years behind without a second thought, I am reminded how quickly life is changing. It was not so long ago that you were my pink, little baby, riding on my hip and loudly expressing your opinions. It was not so long ago that you were the wild toddler, running to me with skinned knees and bruises. It was not so long ago that you were sick; wandering around with dark, sunken eyes; resting in my arms when seizures had sapped all strength from your body, teetering on the brink of death and eternity.

As you began to walk out the door today, I noticed your hair was wild again. Didn't I just brush it two minutes ago? Have you been wrestling with your brothers already this morning? You wiggled through the second brushing of the morning, and as I fixed your piggy-tail, I gave the right side of your head one extra gentle touch. Though your scar is not easily visible, it is something I see and feel often in my heart. It reminds me of the label you wear in my mind that reads: Prognosis: Uncertain.

I always will be tempted to over-protect you, my fragile child. It is hard to let you go, to accept that you are moving on to a new stage of independence. Part of me wants to be your gardener always, to stay with you in our safe little greenhouse, tending to you and soaking up the sunshine with you every day. But that is not my job, nor is it what you need on this day. You are blooming, not withering, and you are strong enough to go out into the elements.

My beautiful flower, your warm, safe greenhouse will be waiting for you when school is over. Mommy will keep the boys from your teddy-bear blanket and your buddies, just as you asked. I will have the chocolate milk ready and waiting when you burst through the doors this afternoon. God will be with you my dear, just as He always has been. Rejoice and blossom!

Sunshine has a way of making us forget, of bringing joy into the present moment, and melting away the ice of the past. Aggie now has life bursting from her and flowing uninterrupted by seizures. She is strong, healthy, and embracing her new independence and good health. Her heart has grown to love her classmates and teachers just as she loves her own family, as everyone knows by the deluge of "beautiful pictures" she pours on them all constantly. She is, once again, a party-starter and a joy-bringer.

After Aggie's surgery, when I allowed myself to believe she was really her healthy self once again, I wanted to be restored, too. I wanted to be the mommy I was before my baby got sick. I wanted to return to the days when I was strong and cheerful, when I really thought summer would last forever. But her scar is still there, and I cannot forget. The flower that blooms in the sun today might shrivel and turn into dust at any moment.

Aggie's sparkling joy disappeared after school when she bumped heads with her brother during a tickle fight. I held her as she covered my shoulder with tears, and smiled a little, because she is still a child. She still needs cheering up when her day is ruined by a skinned knee or hurt feelings. She is still afraid of the dark. She hugged me tightly and wiped her nose on my shirt when she was done crying. "Aggie!" I complained, and she giggled as she ran away in the sunshine.

I, too, am afraid of the dark. Yet my Savior gently calls, **"Let the little children come to me." (Matthew 19:14)**

Appendix: On Being Loved in the Waiting Room

As I think back to our days of waiting rooms and hospital smells, I remember the little things that helped carry us through. I remember the meals, prayers, phone calls, cards and emails. Each small gift nourished our family as we pressed on, minute by minute. God used many people to help us realize that suffering did not mean that we were unloved, only that we were suffering.

There were other things that helped me through, too; things I did not know to ask for, things that I did not even know that I needed, until I received them and was blessed. This is how I would have asked, had I know how to do so. Perhaps these words will help you show God's compassion to another family who is hurting.

Just be with me

It is not fun to be the person or family that reminds everyone of such an enormously sad thing. Some people withdrew, and I understood, knowing that it was usually those who were carrying too much grief already to take on mine as well. Some loved us through it, even though it hurt them to do so—love in a hospital room means sharing worry and grief. Those who were willing to have their hearts ache along with ours were pictures of grace and compassion to me.

Pick up the things I am dropping

Do you know what I am forgetting while I am here with my baby? Perhaps you can help with that. Show love to my healthy kids. Make dinner for my husband. Mow the lawn. Take over the Sunday School class I agreed to teach before everything fell apart.

Let me hide behind technology if I need to

Especially when Aggie had her intensive testing done and we were considering surgery, it became utterly exhausting to me to talk on the phone. I simply did not have the strength to share the details over and over again, to "keep it together" so that the person on the other end of the phone did not have to worry too much about how I was handling everything. I was suffering, and it was all I could do to put one foot in front of the other and keep doing what was in front of me. I blogged when I could, but had very little to say to people by phone. I appreciated that people seemed to understand that.

Take charge of little details

Someone tell me where I left my keys, and remind me to eat something. Someone decide for me what it is I might like to eat, and set it in front of me.

Remind me that other things are happening in life

During the weeks at Cleveland, I remember feeling like our world had become so small. Everything was Aggie's condition, everything was hospital and worry and trial. Yet some who shared our grief were bold enough to share bits of their normal lives with me, and I was surprised at how I appreciated that. A funny story about what someone's kid did that day, news from home or school that had nothing to do with us were blessed reminders that life was still going on outside the hospital, and I could hope to join that world again someday. I had wanted to talk about something else, even just for a minute, but I had no idea what else there could be other than my sick child.

Acknowledge my pain and remind me of Hope

Don't deny my pain with clichés, but look it full in the face, and then tell me that Truth is still Truth. Tell me what I already know, give me scripture and hymns, things I have heard a thousand times—I need to hear them again. Nothing fancy or profound, just speak the basic faith we share: Suffering is awful, but temporary, because Jesus loves us. Even when we hurt, we are safe in His love for us.

How precious is your steadfast love, O God!
The children of mankind take refuge
in the shadow of your wings.
They feast on the abundance of your house,
and you give them drink from the river of your delights.
For with you is the fountain of life;
in your light do we see light.
(Ps 36:7-9)

Endnotes

1   Acker, J.W., The Lutheran Book of Prayer (St. Louis: Concordia Publishing House, 2005) 211.

2   The Lutheran Hymnal (St Louis: Concordia Publishing House, 1941) #345 verse 1

3   Lutheran Service Book (St Louis: Concordia Publishing House, 2006) #370 verse 1

4   Ibid., verse 2

5   Ps 124:8

6   The Lutheran Hymnal (St Louis: Concordia Publishing House, 1941) #345 verse 2

7   Lutheran Service Book (St Louis: Concordia Publishing House, 2006) 192.

8   Ibid. 186.

For more by Emily Cook
including the latest on Aggie
please visit
http://www.weakandloved.com

Made in the USA
Lexington, KY
23 May 2013